Minnie Moore-Willson

The Seminoles of Florida

Minnie Moore-Willson

The Seminoles of Florida

ISBN/EAN: 9783337112981

Printed in Europe, USA, Canada, Australia, Japan

Cover: Foto ©Suzi / pixelio.de

More available books at **www.hansebooks.com**

THE SEMINOLES

OF

FLORIDA

BY

MINNIE MOORE-WILLSON

AMERICAN PRINTING HOUSE
1019 Cherry Street
Philadelphia
1896

PREFACE.

That there is yet a tribe, or are tribes of Indians in Florida is a fact unknown to a large part of the people of this country; there are even students of history who have scarcely known it. These people, driven, about seventy or more years ago, into the dreary everglades of that Southern Peninsula, have kept themselves secluded from the ever encroaching white population of the State. Only occasionally would a very small number visit a town or a city to engage in traffic. They have had no faith in the white man, or the white man's government. They have aimed to be peaceful, but have, with inveterate purpose, abstained from intercourse with any of the agencies of our government. My friends, Mr. and Mrs. J. M. Willson, Jr., of Kissimmee, Florida, have found their way to a large degree of confidence in the hearts of this people. They have learned something of their history, and have studied their manner of life, their character and habits.

Mr. Willson has been allowed, and invited to go with some of their men on familiar hunting expeditions. He has seen them in the swamps, in their homes, and in their general life environments. He has been admitted to their confidence and friendship. He has consequently become deeply interested in them. Mrs. Willson also has become acquainted with some of their chief personages. Both have learned to sympathize with these Indians in their hardships, and in their treatment at the hands of the white race.

Mrs. Willson began to write about them and her writing has grown into a book; and she has been encouraged to give this book to the world, in the hope that the attention of good people may be drawn toward them, and that at last a true interest may be awakened in their moral and material well-being. They are truly an interesting people, living, although secluded, almost at our doors.

Mrs. Willson has written earnestly, enthusiastically, and lovingly regarding them, and it is to be hoped that a new interest may soon be taken in them both by the churches and the government, and that they may soon enter upon new realizations, and be encouraged to place a confidence in the white race to which, until quite recently, they have been utter strangers.

Mr. Willson has prepared the vocabulary. The words and phrases here given have been gathered by him in the course of eight or ten years of friendly intercourse with members of the tribe. They have assisted him in getting the true Indian or Seminole word and in finding its signification. Old Chief Tallahassee has been especially and kindly helpful; so has Captain Tom Tiger. This vocabulary of this peculiar Indian tribe, though not complete, ought to prove helpful to those who are interested in the languages of the people who roamed the forests of this great land before it became the home and the domain of those who now live and rule in it.

This book, in its first part, gives some account of the earlier years of the Seminole history. In the second part the reader is introduced to the later and present state of things and facts regarding them.

In the third part is found the vocabulary—a number of Seminole words, phrases and names, with their interpretation into our own tongue.

This little book is given to the world in the hope that it will be found both interesting and valuable to many readers.

R. BRADEN MOORE.

Vineland, N. J.

CONTENTS..

Contents.

Part First

Facts of Earlier Days.

THE history of the American Indian is a very iliad of tragedy. From the day Columbus made the first footprints of the European in the damp sands of Cat Island, the story of the original owners of fair America has been full of melancholy, and fills with its dark pages every day of a quartet of centuries.

Columbus describes the innocent happiness of these people—"They were no wild savages, but very gentle and courteous," he says, "without knowing what evil is, without stealing, without killing." They gave to him a new world for Castile and Leon, while in exchange he gave to them "some glass beads and little red caps." The tragedy of the new world began when we find this same admiral writing to the Spanish majesties that he would be able to furnish them with gold, cotton, spices, and slaves—"slaves! as many as their Highnesses shall command to be shipped"; and thus, this land, a paradise of almost primeval loveliness, was transformed into a land of cruel bondage, desolation and death.

History scarcely records an instance when hospi-

tality was not extended by the red man to our first
explorers. Swift canoes shot out from the shaded
shores, filled with men clad in gorgeous mantles, and,
in broken accents, their greeting was "Welcome!"
"Come, see the people from Heaven," they cried, but
were soon destined to believe they were from a very
different region. Amid the salutes of artillery, the
music of trumpets and the cheers of thousands of Castilians did De Soto march upon the native population.
Greyhounds of wonderful fleetness, and bloodhounds of
largest size and ferocity were brought to be turned
loose upon the savages; also handcuffs, chains and neck
collars to secure them. From old Spanish accounts we
conclude that the Indian population of De Soto's time
was very large, and that the natives were in a higher
state of civilization than at any later period; that their
speech, though brief, was chaste, unaffected, and evinced
a generous sentiment. Cortez found the Aztecs and
their dependencies challenging comparison with the
proudest nations of the world, and in their barbarous
magnificence rivaling the splendors of the Orient.
Advanced in the arts, dwelling in cities, and living
under a well organized government, they were happy
in their position and circumstances.

Notwithstanding the hospitable treatment shown
by the natives to the newcomers, the Castilians
destroyed them by the thousands. One explorer after
another wrote of these friendly people in the new land.
"They are very liberal," says the narrator, "for they

give what they have." Sir Ralph Lane describes the
welcome by the natives, who came with "Tobacco,
Corne and furs and kindly gestures to be friends with
the strange white men, etc., etc., but adds, "the Indians
stole a Silver Cup, wherefore we burnt their Towne
and spoylt their Corne," etc., etc.

The time will soon be over for the study of the
Aborigines of America. We have in 250 years wasted
them from uncounted numbers to a scattering population of only about 275,000, while in the same length
of time a cargo of dusky slaves from the African shores
have become a people of millions, slaves no longer, but
protected citizens. In the redskin, whom we have
dispossessed of his native rights, we recognize no
equality; yet the descendant of the barbarous black,
whose tribe on the Golden Coast still trembles before a
fetish, may now sit at the desk of Clay or Calhoun.
Truly the tangled threads of modern morals are hard to
unravel.

The first explorers made captives of the Indians,
and carried them in irons to Spain, where they were
sold as slaves to the Spanish grandees. Two hundred
years later the people of Carolina sought to enslave
those among them. The red men rebelled at the sub-
jection, and in order to escape bondage, began to make
their way to the "Indian country"—the present site of
Georgia. African bondsmen soon followed the example
of the Indian captives, and in time continued their
journey to Florida.

*In the attempts to recapture runaway slaves is
based the primeval cause of the Seminole Wars.*

ORIGIN OF TROUBLES.

The history of the Seminoles of Florida begins
with their separation from the Creeks of Georgia as
early as 1750—the name Seminole, in Indian dialect
meaning wild wanderers or runaways. Seacoffee, their
leader, conducted them to the territory of Florida, then
under the Spanish colonial policy. Here, they sought
the protection of Spanish laws, refused in all after
times to be represented in Creek councils, elected their
own chiefs, and became, in all respects, a separate
tribe.

To-day the Seminoles of Florida are only a frail
remnant of that powerful tribe of Osceola's day. Their
history presents a character, a power and a romance
that impels respect and an acknowledgment of their
superiority. Of the private life of the Seminole less
is known, perhaps, than of any other band in the
United States. His life has been one long struggle for
a resting place; he has fought for home, happy hunting
grounds and the burial place of his fathers. At present we can only see a race whose destiny says—extinction.

The wilds of Florida became a home for these
Indians as well as for the fugitive negro slaves of the
Southern States. The Indian and the negro refugee,
settling in the same sections, became friendly, and in

time some of their people intermarried. The same American spirit that refused to submit to "Taxation without Representation," was strong in the breast of the Seminole, and Florida, belonging to Spain, afforded him a retreat for his independent pursuits. Subject only to the Spanish crown, the exiles found a home, safe from the inexorable slave catchers. The Seminoles were now enjoying liberty, and a social solitude, and refused to make a treaty with the colonial government, or with the Creeks from whom they had separated. One demand after another was made upon the Spanish government at St. Augustine for the return of the fugitives, which was always rejected. African slaves continued to flee from their masters to find refuge with the exiles and the Indians. They were eagerly received, and kindly treated, and soon admitted to a footing of equality. The growing demand for slaves in the southern colonies now made the outlook serious, and from the attempts to compel the return of the negroes grew the first hostilities.

One of the first communications ever sent to Congress after it met was by the Georgia colony, stating that "a large number of continental troops would be required to prevent the slaves from deserting their masters." But in that momentous year of 1776, Congress had more important duties on hand, and it was not until 1790 that a treaty was entered into between the Creeks and the United States. In this treaty, the Creeks, now at enmity with the Seminoles, agreed to restore the slaves of the Georgia planters who had taken refuge among them. The Seminoles refused to recognize the treaty—they were no longer a part of the Creeks, they resided in Florida and considered themselves subject only to the crown of Spain. One can readily believe that the Spanish authorities encouraged their independence. Legally the exiles had become a free people.

The Creeks now found themselves utterly unable to comply with their treaty. The planters of Georgia began to press the government for the return of their fugitive slaves. Secretary Knox, foreseeing the difficulty of recovering runaway slaves, wrote to the President advising that the Georgia people be paid by the government for the loss of their bondmen. The message was tabled, and until 1810 the Seminoles and negroes lived in comparative peace.

The people of Georgia, now seeing the only apparent way to obtain possession of their slaves would be by the annexation of Florida, began to petition for this, but the United States, feeling less interest in slave catching than did the state of Georgia, manipulated affairs so slowly that Georgia determined to redress her own grievances, entered Florida and began hostilities. The United States was too much occupied with the war with Great Britain to take cognizance of Indian troubles in a Spanish province, hence the Georgia intruders met with defeat. For a short time after these hostilities ceased the Seminoles and their allies enjoyed

prosperity, cultivated their fields, told their traditions
and sang their rude lays around their peaceful camp
fires. Seventy-five years had passed since their ancestors had found a home in Florida, and it was hard
for them to understand the claims of the southern
planters.

The year 1816 found the Seminoles at peace with
the white race. In a district inhabited by many of the
Indians on the Appalachicola river was Blount's Fort.

The fort, although Spanish property, was reported
as an "asylum for runaway negroes." General Jackson,
now in military command, ordered the "blowing up of
the fort and the return of the negroes to their rightful
owners." The exiles knowing little of scientific warfare believed themselves safe in this retreat; and when
in 1816 an expedition under Col. Duncan L. Clinch
was planned, the hapless Indians and Negroes un-
knowingly rushed into the very jaws of death. A
shot from a gunboat exploded the magazines and destroyed the garrison. History records that of 334 souls
in the fort, 270 were *instantly killed!* The groans of
the wounded and dying, the savage war whoops of the
Indians inspired the most fiendish revenge in the
hearts of those who escaped, and marks the beginning
of the *first Seminole War.*

Savage vengeance was now on fire, and "Blount's
Fort" became the magnetic war cry of the Seminole
chiefs as they urged their warriors to retaliation. This
barbarous sacrifice of innocent women and children

conducted by a christian nation against a helpless race, and for no other cause than that their ancestors, one hundred years before, had been born in slavery, marks a period of cruelty, one of the most wanton in the history of our nation.

The inhuman way in which the massacre was conducted was never published at large; nor does the War Department have any record of the taking of Blount's Fort, as is shown by the following:

"An examination of the records of this Department has been made, but no information bearing upon the subject of the taking of Blount's Fort, Florida, in the year 1816, has been found of record."
"By authority of the Secretary of War."
"F. C. AINSWORTH,
Colonel, U. S. Army, Chief of Office."
"WASHINGTON, July 25, 1895."

History does not dwell on the cruel treatment the Indians received from the United States authorities during the Seminole Wars, yet pages of our National Library are devoted to the barbarity of the Seminoles. There are two sides to every question, and it is only what the Indian does to the white man that is published, and not what the white man does to the Indian.

The facts show that instead of seeking to injure the people of the United States, the Seminoles were, and have been, only anxious to be free from all contact with our government. In no official correspondence is there any reference made to acts of hostility by the Indians, prior to the massacre at Blount's Fort.

But Floridians, who had urged the war with the hope of seizing and enslaving the maroons of the interior, now saw their own plantations laid waste, villages abandoned to the enemy, and families suffering for bread. The war had been commenced for an ignoble purpose—to re-enslave fellow-men—and taught that every violation of justice is followed by appropriate penalties.

Few of the people of the United States knew the true cause of the war, nor the real inwardness of the purposes of those in command, as history and official documents show that affairs were in the hands of the Executive rather than in those of Congress. The first war was in itself an act of hostility to the King of Spain; yet nothing was gained by our government except possession of part of the fugitives. Military forces could not pursue the Indians into the fastnesses of the Everglades, and after two years of bloodshed and expenditure of thousands of dollars, peace was in a manner restored, and the army was withdrawn without any treaty being signed.

EFFORTS AT INDIAN REMOVAL.

The Indians had set the American government at defiance. The slaves of Southern States continued to run away, taking refuge with the exiles and Seminoles;

the slave-holders of Georgia became more clamorous than ever. The Spanish crown could not protect herself from the invasion of the Americans when in pursuit of runaway negroes. She had seen her own subjects massacred, her forts destroyed or captured, and her rights as a nation insulted by an American army. In 1819, by a combination of force and negotiation, Florida was purchased from Spain for $5,000,000.

Thus the Seminoles were brought under the dominion they so much dreaded. Slave-holders once more petitioned to the United States for aid in the capture of their escaped property. The United States, foiled in their treaty with the Creeks, now recognized the Seminoles as a distinct tribe, and invited their chiefs to meet our commissioners and negotiate a treaty. The Seminoles agreed in this treaty to take certain reservations assigned them, the United States covenanting *to take the Florida Indians under her care and to afford them protection against all persons whatsoever, and to restrain and prevent all white persons from hunting, settling or otherwise intruding upon said lands.*

By this treaty all their cultivated lands were given up to the whites, and the Seminoles retired to the interior. Once more this long persecuted people found refuge, but it was only for a short time. The value of slaves in States North, caused slave catchers with chains and bloodhounds to enter Florida. They seized the slaves of the Indians, stole their horses and cattle and depredated their property. With such a violation of the treaty, renewed hostilities were inevitable.

The Indians petitioned for redress, but received none. Affairs grew worse until 1828, when the idea of emigration for the Indians was submitted to the chiefs. After much persuasion, a few of the tribal leaders were induced to visit the Western country. They found the climate cold, and a land where "snow covers the ground, and frosts chill the bodies of men," and on general principles, Arkansas a delusion and a snare. The chiefs had been told they might go and see for themselves, but that they were not obliged to move unless they *liked the land*. In their speech to the Commissioner they said: " We are not willing to go. If our tongues say 'yes', our hearts cry 'no.' You would send us among bad Indians, with whom we could never be at rest. Even our horses were stolen by the Pawnees, and we were obliged to carry our packs on our backs. We are not hungry for other lands— we are happy here. If we are torn from these forests our heartstrings will snap." Notwithstanding the opposition to a treaty, by a system of coercion, a part of the chiefs were induced to sign, and fifteen undoubted Seminole cross-marks were affixed to the paper. This was not enough, according to Indian laws, to compel emigration. The stipulations read, "prepare to emigrate West, and *join the Creeks*." There was no agreement that their negroes should accompany them, and they refused to move. Expecting a tribe which had lived at enmity with the Creeks since their separation in 1750 to emigrate and live with them, was but to put weapons into their hands, and did not coincide with the ideas of the Seminoles.

The United States prepared to execute—not a redskin was ready, and troops were sent. The Indians began immediately to gather their crops, remove the squaws and piccaninnies to places of safety, secure war equipments,—in short, prepare for battle.

It was a question of wonderment many times among the officers how the Indians procured their ammunition in such quantities, and how they kept from actual starvation. Hidden as they were in their strong fortresses—the fastnesses of the swamps—many believed that they would be starved out, and would either stand a fair field fight or sue for peace. An old Florida settler who carried his rifle through seven years of Indian warfare, explains the mystery. He says: "The Indians had been gathering powder and lead for years, ever since the time Chief Neamathla made his treaty with General Jackson. Besides, Cuban fishing smacks were always bringing it in and trading with the redskins for hides and furs. As for provisions, they had their 'Koontie' flour, the acorn of the live oak, which is fair eating when roasted, and the cabbage of the palmetto tree. For meat, the woods were full of it. Deer and bear were abundant, to say nothing of small game, such as wild turkey, turtle and squirrel." The Seminoles at this time, 1834, owned,

perhaps, two hundred slaves, their people had intermarried with the maroons, and in fighting for these
allies they were fighting for blood and kin. To remove
the Indians and not the Negroes was a difficult thing to
do. The Seminoles, now pressed by the United States
troops, committed depredations upon the whites; bloody
tragedies occurred, and the horrors of the second Seminole War were chronicled throughout the land.

THE MASSACRE OF GENERAL THOMPSON AND OF DADES FORCES.

It was now that the young and daring warrior,
Osceola, came into prominence. He had recently
married the daughter of an Indian chief, but whose
mother was the descendant of a fugitive slave. By
slave-holding laws, the child follows the condition of the
mother, and Osceola's wife was called an African slave.
The young warrior, in company with his wife, visited
the trading post of Fort King for the purpose of buy-
ing supplies. While there the young wife was seized
and carried off in chains. Osceola became wild with
grief and rage, and no knight of cavalier days ever
showed more valor than did this Spartan Indian in the
attempts to recapture his wife. For this he was arrested by order of General Thompson and put in irons.
With the cunning of the Indian, Osceola affected peni-
tence and was released—but revenge was uppermost in
his soul. The war might succeed or fail for all he cared—
to avenge the capture of his wife was his every

thought. For weeks he secreted himself, watching an opportunity to murder General Thompson and his friends. No influence could dissuade him from his bloody purpose. Discovering General Thompson and Lieutenant Smith taking a walk one day, Osceola, yelling the war cry sprang like a mountain cat from his hiding place and murdered both men.

His work of vengeance was now complete, and almost as wild as a Scandanavian Saga was the fight he now gave our generals for nearly two years.

While Osceola lay in wait for General Thompson, plans were being completed which resulted in the Dade Massacre.

The enmity of the Indian is proverbial, and when we reflect that for fifty years the persecutions by the whites had been "talked" in their camps, that the massacre of Blount's Fort was still unavenged, that within memory fathers and mothers had been torn, moaning and groaning from their midst, to be sold into bondage; with their savage natures all on fire for retaliation, no vengeance was too terrible.

Hostilities around Fort King, now the present site of Ocala, becoming severe, General Clinch ordered the troops under Major Dade, then stationed at Fort Brooke, (Tampa) to march to his assistance. Neither officers nor soldiers were acquainted with the route— and a negro guide was detailed to lead them. This unique character was Louis Pacheo, a negro slave belonging to an old Spanish family, then living near

Fort Brooke. The slave was well acquainted with the Indians, spoke the Seminole tongue fluently. He was reported by his master, as *faithful*, *intelligent* and *trustworthy*, and was perfectly familiar with the route to Fort King.

The affair of Dades Massacre is without a parallel in the history of Indian war-fare. Of the 110 souls, who, with flying flags and sounding bugles merrily responded to General Clinch's order, but two lived to describe in after years the tragic scenes. One was Private Clark, of the 2nd artillery, who, wounded and sick crawled on his hands and knees a distance of sixty miles to Fort Brooke. The other was Louis Pacheco, the only person of the command who *escaped without a wound*.

The assault was made shortly after the troops crossed the Withlacoochee river, in a broad expanse of open pine woods, with here and there clumps of palmettoes and tall wire grass. The Indians are supposed to have out-numbered the command, two to one, and at a given signal, as the troops marched gayly along, a volley of shot was poured into their number. The "gallant Dade" was the first to fall pierced by a ball from Micanopy's musket, who was the King of the Seminole nation. A breastwork was attempted by the soldiers, but only served as a retreat for a short time ; the hot missiles from the Indians soon laid the last man motionless, and the slaughter was at an end.

On February 20, 1836, almost two months after

the massacre, the dead bodies of the officers and soldiers were found just as they had fallen on that fatal
day. History is corroborated by old settlers, who say
"that the dead were in no way pillaged; articles the
most esteemed by savages were untouched, their
watches were found in the pockets, and money, in silver and gold, was left to decay with its owner—a lesson
to all the world—a testimony that the Indians were
not fighting for plunder! The arms and ammunition
were all that had been taken, except the uniform coat
of Major Dade." Their motive was higher and purer
—they were fighting for their rights, their homes, their
very existence.

What became of the negro guide? History records
that Louis, knowing the time and place at which the
attack was to be made, separated himself from the
troops. As soon as the fire commenced, he joined the
Indians and negroes, and lent his efforts in carrying
forth the work of death. An extract printed over forty
years ago describes the character of the negro Louis.
It reads as follows:

"'The life of the slave Louis is perhaps the most
romantic of any man now living. Born and reared a
slave, he found time to cultivate his intellect—was fond
of reading; and while gentlemen in the House of Representatives were engaged in discussing the value of
his bones and sinews, he could probably speak and
write more languages with ease and facility than any
member of that body. In revenge for the oppression
to which he was subjected, he conceived the purpose

of sacrificing a regiment of white men who were engaged in the support of slavery. This object effected, he asserted his own natural right to freedom, joined his brethren, and made bloody war upon the enemies of liberty. For two years he was the steady companion of Coacoochee, or, as he was afterwards called, "Wild Cat," who subsequently became the most warlike chief in Florida. They traversed the forests of that territory together, wading through swamps and everglades, groping their way through hommocks, and gliding over prairies. For two years they stood shoulder to shoulder in every battle; shared their victories and defeats together; and, when General Jessup had pledged the faith of the nation that all Indians who would surrender should be protected in the enjoyment of their slaves, Wild Cat appeared at headquarters, followed by Louis, whom he claimed as his *property*, under slaveholding law, as he said he had *captured* him at the time of Dade's defeat."

Following Louis Pacheo's career, we find him sharing the fortunes of Wild Cat in the Indian Territory. Subsequently, Wild Cat, with a few followers, Louis among the number, emigrated to Mexico. Fiftyseven years passed from the date of the Dade massacre, when Louis Pacheo, venerable and decrepit, once more appeared on Florida soil. The old negro, longing for the scenes of his youth, returned to end his days in the hospitable home of his "old missus," who yet resides in Jacksonville, Florida. In his confession he claims to be innocent of the charge of betraying the troops, and asserts that he was forced into remaining with the

Indians. The vagaries of a childish mind may account for his diversion from well-established history. The old slave lived for three years after his return to Florida, and died in January, 1895, at the age of 95 years.

A DISHONORED TREATY.

The tragic news of the Dade Massacre convinced the United States that war had commenced in real earnest. From this time on, skirmish after skirmish ensued, bloody murders were committed by the redskins, thousands of dollars were being expended by our government, and the white population of Florida was in a suffering condition. The Indians were not suffering for food. The chameleon-like character of the war prevented any certainty of success. General Jessup, considerably chagrined, wrote to Washington for permission to resign both the glory and baton of his command.

There could scarcely arise a more painful theme, or one presenting a stranger variety of aspects, as it whirled scathing and bloodily along, than did the Indian War. Yet it is a remarkable fact that no Seminole warrior had ever surrendered, even to superior numbers. Our military forces had learned what a hydra-headed monster the war really was, and attempts were again made to induce emigration. The horrors of the Dade Massacre and of Fort King had reached the world. General Jessup sought negotiations, but found the same difficulties to encounter as before, viz.: that the chiefs would not enter into an agreement that did not guarantee equal rights to their allies as to the Indians. Official documents show that General Jessup agreed that " the Seminoles and their allies who come in and emigrate West, shall be secure in their lives and property ; that their negroes, their bona fide property, shall accompany them West, and that their cattle and ponies shall be paid for by the United States." The Indians, under these terms, now prepared to emigrate. History records that even Osceola avowed his intention to accompany them. Every preparation was made to emigrate, and a tract of land near Tampa was selected on which to gather their people. Hundreds of Indians and negroes encamped here. Vessels were anchored to transport them to their new homes. Peace was apparent everywhere, and the war declared at an end. At this point a new difficulty arose. Slaveholders became indignant at the stipulations of the treaty, and once more commenced to seize negroes. The Seminoles, thinking themselves betrayed, with clear conceptions of justice, fled to their former fastnesses in the interior, and once more determined to defend their liberty.

In the violation of the treaty, to use General Jessup's words, *all was lost !!*

All the vengeance of the Indian was again aroused, and the wild Seminole war-cry, "Yohoehee! yohoehee," again broke through the woods.

As–se–he–ho–lar, The Rising Sun, or Osceola.

The fame of Osceola now reached the farthermost
corner of the land.   His name, signifying Rising Sun,*
seemed prophetic, and he became at once the warrior
of the Ocklawaha—the hero of the Seminoles.   The
youngest of the chiefs, he possessed a magnetism that
Cyrus might have envied, and in a manner truly majestic led his warriors where he chose.

In the personal reminiscences of an old Florida
settler, in describing Osceola, he says, "I consider him
one of the greatest men this country ever produced.
He was a great man, and a curious one, too; but few
people knew him well enough to appreciate his worth.
I was raised within ten miles of his home, and it was
he who gave me my first lessons in woodcraft.   He was
a brave and generous foe, and always protected women
and children.   An act of kindness was never forgotten
by him.   Osceola had received a favor from one of the
officers who led the battle of the Withlacoochee.   Ob-
serving him in the front ranks, he instantly gave or-
ders that this man should be spared, but every other
officer should be cut down.   Osceola's father was an
English trader named Powell, and his mother the
daughter of a chief known as Sallie Marie—a woman
very small in stature, and with high cheek-bones.   Os-

---

* Catlin and others give "the black drink " as the signification of Osceola,
or Asseola, from the man's capacity for that drink.   Asseola was doubtless the
original and true name.   But "Asse" or "hasse," in the present Seminole
tongue, means "the sun."   This, with the affix "ola," or "he-ho-lar," would
mean "the rising sun" rather than "the black drink."

Sister-in-law of Osceola, 85 years old, and her great great-grand-children.

ceola lacked this peculiarity, and was one of the finest-
looking men I ever saw. His carriage was erect and
lofty, his motion quick, and he had an air of hauteur
in his countenance which arose from his elevated pride
of soul. I tell you, he was a great man; education
would have made him the equal of Napoleon. He
hated slavery as only such a nature as his could hate.
He was Indian to the heart, and proud of his ancestry.
He had too much white blood in him to yield to the
cowardly offers of the government, and had he not been
captured, the Seminole War would have been a more
lasting one than it was. I could talk all day about
Osceola," remarked the old Captain, as he drew a sigh.
" Did the Indians take scalps, Captain?" "'Take scalps?
—well, yes, if Osceola wasn't around. He was too
much of a white man to allow it himself."

The admixture of Caucasian blood, stimulated the
ambition of Osceola's Indian nature; his book learning,
together with the teachings of nature, made him able
to cope with the most learned. Living until he was
almost twelve years of age in the Creek confederacy of
Georgia, his youthful mind received deep and lasting
impressions from Tecumseh's teachings. To these
teachings, as well as the blood he inherited from his
Spartan ancestors was due, no doubt, his supremacy in
the Seminole war. In the manner in which he led the
Seminoles may be seen the influence of the great
Shawnee. Osceola's power was in his strong personal
magnetism; he swayed his warriors with a look—a

shout of command produced an electric effect upon all. He was a hero among his people, he was feared and dreaded by our officers. In this day, as we study his life and character, we must recognize in the young Seminole fighter, the greatest of chiefs, the boldest of warriors.

Interviewing old settlers who well remember events of those stiring times, one finds the heroic part of Osceola's character to have been not overdrawn in history. The Seminole chief, Charles Omatla, was an ally of the whites, and was attacked and murdered by Osceola's warriors. On his body was found gold, which Osceola forbade his men to touch, but with his own hands he threw the gold himself as far as he could hurl it, saying "it is the price of the red man's blood."

Osceola's pride was majestic; he was imperious, full of honor, but with the quickness of the Indian he noted the path to popular favor. His power was recognized by the officers. "Talk after talk," with the Indians was the order of the times. It was at one of these meetings that Osceola in the presence of the commissioners attracted attention by saying, "this is the only treaty I will ever make with the whites," at the same time drawing his knife and striking it into the table before him. The cause of this outburst was that the stipulations of the treaty guaranteed no protection to the allies. He was arrested for his insolence, but was released on a compromise. His vengeance became more terrible than ever, and in defiance "Yohoehee" echoed through the woods and "war to the knife" was resumed. It was now that the daring chief made the bold and well conducted assault against the fort at Micanopy. A short time after, this savage hero performed a piece of strategy before unheard of in the annals of war. Surrounded by two armies of equal strength with his own, he carried away his warriors without leaving a trace of his retreat. That host of Indian braves melted out of sight as if by magic, and our disappointed generals could not but agree that a disciplined army was not adapted to the work of surprising Indians. They were learning to recognize the character of the men our nation had to deal with.

The Indian method is to decoy by a broad plain trail, then at a certain distance the foremost of the band makes a high long step—leaves the trail and alighting on the tip of his toe, carefully smoothes out the brushed blades behind him. The rest of the band go on a few yards farther and make their exit the same way, and so on till the end is reached. Many times our troops made long night marches to find—what? nothing but a few smouldering camp fires.

The war waged on in defiance of the power of a mighty nation—a nation that had said to old King George, "attend to your own affairs" and he obeyed.

One is half tempted to believe that a kind of dark fatality controlled our army's best planned movements.

After months of warfare, Osceola in company with Wild Cat and other chiefs was persuaded, under a flag of truce, to meet General Hernandez on October 21, 1837, at St. Augustine. With that grave dignity characteristic of the red man, dressed in costume becoming their station, with as courtly a bearing as ever graced kings, heralding their white flags they approached the place of meeting.

History verifies the Seminole account of this blot on our nation, that as the officers approached, they asked of Osceola: "Are you prepared to deliver up the negroes taken from the citizens? Why have you not surrendered them as promised by your chief Cohadjo?"

According to history, this promise had been made by a sub-chief and without the consent of the tribe. A signal, preconcerted, was at this moment given and armed soldiers rushed in and made prisoners of the chiefs.

An account of this violated honor, recently given by the venerable John S. Masters, of St. Augustine, Florida, is opportune at this point. The old soldier in speaking of the affair said, " I was one of the party sent out to meet Osceola when he was coming to St. Augustine under a flag of truce." "Did you honor that truce?" was asked. " Did we? No sir; no sooner was he safe within our lines than the order to seize him, kill if necessary, was given, and one of the soldiers knocked him down with the butt of his musket. He was then bound and we brought him to Fort Mar-

ion and he was put in the dungeon. We were all out-
raged by the cowardly way he was betrayed into being
captured."

At this violation of the sanctity of the white flag
our officers wrote: "The end justifies the means—they
have made fools of us too often."

The foul means used to capture the young Seminole leader was not blessed by victory, as a continu-
ance of the bloody war for five years proved that the
God of justice was not wholly on the white man's side.
The stain on our national honor will last as long as we
have a history. Osceola, with the other chiefs was
confined for a short time in St. Augustine, but the
daring savage was too valuable a prize to trust on
Florida territory, and he was taken to Fort Moultrie
where he died January 30, 1838, at the age of thirty-
four years.

Thoroughly and thrillingly dramatic was the death
scene of the noble Osceola as given by Dr. Weedon his
attending surgeon. Confinement no doubt hastened
his death, and his proud spirit sank under the doom of
prison life. He seemed to feel the approach of death,
and about half an hour before the summons came he
signified by signs—he could not speak—that he wished
to see the chiefs and officers of the post. Making known
that he wished his full dress, which he wore in time of
war, it was brought him, and rising from his bed he
dressed himself in the insignia of a chief. Exhausted
by these efforts the swelling heart of the tempest-tossed

frame subsided into stillest melancholy. With the death sweat already upon his brow, Osceola laid down a few minutes to recover his strength. Then, rising as before, with gloom dispelled, and a face agleam with smiles, the young warrior reached forth his hand and in dead silence bade each and all the officers and chiefs a last farewell. By his couch knelt his two wives and his little children. With the same oppressive silence he tenderly shook hands with these loved ones. Then signifying his wish to be lowered on his bed, with slow hand he drew from his war belt his scalping knife which he firmly grasped in his right hand, laying it across the the other on his breast. In another moment he smiled away his last breath, without a struggle or a groan. In that death chamber there was not one tearless eye. Friends and foes, alike, wept over the dying chief. Osceola died as he lived—a hero among men.

THE HIDDEN WAR CAMP.

Wild Cat and Cohadjo were allowed to remain in the prison at St. Augustine. Wild Cat feigned sickness and was permitted, under guard, to go to the woods to obtain some roots—with these he reduced his size until he was able to crawl through an aperture that admitted light into the cell. Letting himself down by ropes made of the bedding, a distance of fifty feet, he made his escape, joined his tribe and once more rallied his forces against our army. Latter day critics have questioned the correctness of this bit of written history.

Last winter, during the height of the season, the Ponce de Leon guests enjoyed a unique entertainment. A wealthy tourist made a wager of one hundred dollars that "Wild Cat never could have made his escape through the little window in the old castle." Sergeant Brown accepted the wager and himself performed the feat, to the great delight of the excited spectators.

Our soldiers fighting in an unexplored wilderness, along the dark borders of swamp and morass, crawling many times on hands and knees through the tangled matted underbrush, fighting these children of the forest who knew every inch of their ground could hope for little less than defeat. Even General Jessup in writing to the President said: "We are attempting to remove the Indians when they are not in the way of the white settlers, and when the greater portion of the country is an unexplored wilderness, of the interior of which we are as ignorant as of the interior of China."

By way of illustrating the enormity of the task the government had in subduing the Seminoles, it is only necessary to describe one of the many Indian strongholds in the swamps of Florida. About ten miles from Kissimmee, west by south, is a cypress swamp made by the junction of the Davenport, Reedy and Bonnet creeks. It is an acquatic jungle, full of fallen trees, brush, vines and tangled undergrowth, all darkened by the dense shadows of the tall cypress trees. The surface is covered with water, which, from appearance may be any depth, from six inches to six feet;

this infested with alligators and moccasins would have been an unsurmountable barrier to the white troops.

A few years ago when the Seminoles yet frequented this section for trading purposes, old settlers have seen them coming from the swamp carrying bags of oranges. Interrogations received no answers and white settlers year after year searched for the traditional orange grove, but without success.

So difficult to penetrate and so dangerous to explore is the swamp that it was not until fifty years after the Indians had left their island home that a venturesome hunter, during a very dry season, accidentally discovered the old Seminole camp. The Indian mound, the broken pottery and the long hunted for sweet orange grove were proofs of the old camp. The majestic orange trees laden with golden fruit, were an incentive to further research. With a surveyor working his way, as guided by the point of the compass, this wonderland was explored, and proved to be a complete chain of small hommocks or islands running through from one side of the swamp to the other; the topography of the marsh being such that a skirmish could take place on one side of the jungle and an hour later, by means of the secret route through the swamp, the Indians could be ready for an attack on the other side, while for the troops to reach the same point, by following the only road known to them, it would have required nearly a day's marching. The Indian trail is lost in the almost impenetrable jungle; but the toma-

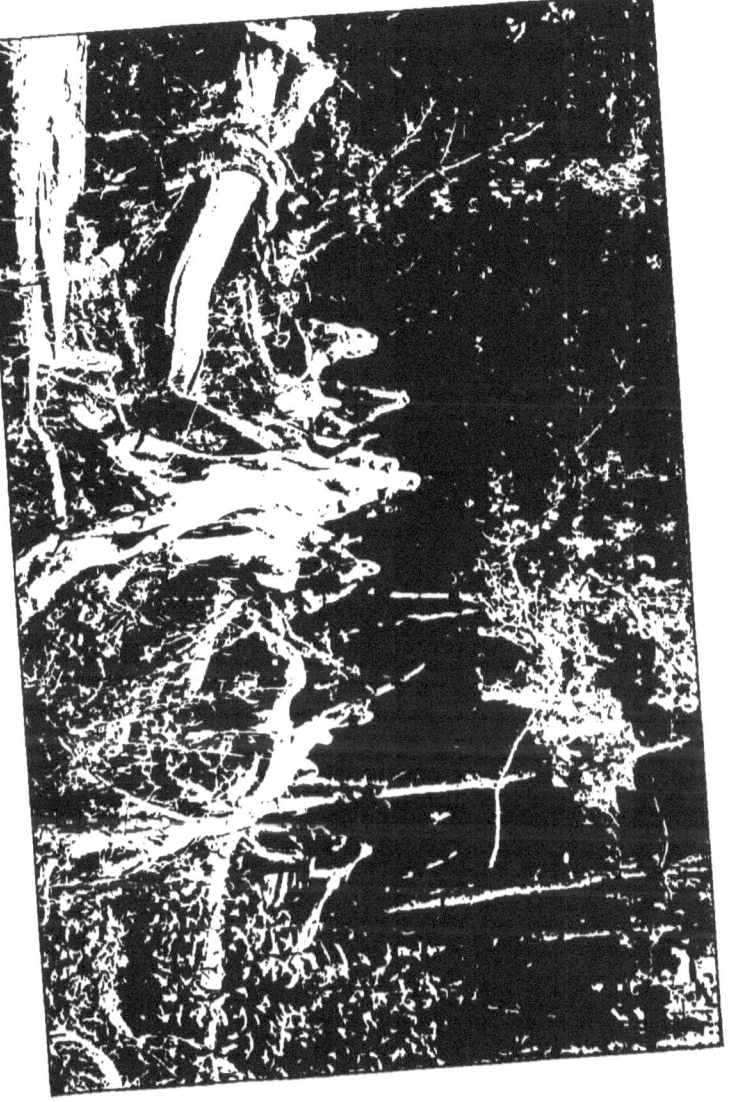

An Indian Retreat During the Seminole War.

hawk blazes are perfectly discernible. The Seminoles held the key to these mysterious islands and in the heart of the great swamps they lived free from any danger of surprise. This retreat must have been a grand rendez-vous for them, as its geographical position was almost central between the principal forts. Lying between Fort Brooke (Tampa) and Fort King (Ocala), within a distance of thirty miles from the scene of the Dade massacre, about forty miles from Fort Mellon, the present site of Sanford, the camp could have been reached in a few hours by Indian runners after spying the movements of the troops at any of the forts. The old government road, over which the soldiers passed in going from Fort Brooke to Fort Mellon, passes so close to the old Indian camping ground that all travel could have been watched by the keen eyed warriors.

WILD CAT AND GENERAL WORTH.

At this period of our national history we are un-able to picture or appreciate the condition of those slave days, when all blacks of Southern States were regarded as the property of the whites. The fear, the torture, the grief suffered by the negroes and half breeds, who had been a people with the Seminoles almost one hundred years, is beyond our conception. When Indian husbands were separated from wives selected from the exiles—when children were torn from their homes and carried to slavery, the vengeance of these persecuted people was constantly alive. Persons of disreputable character—gamblers, horse thieves—were employed as slave catchers and showed no mercy to the helpless victim.

After the violation of the treaty at Tampa, and the capture of Osceola and Wild Cat, under the sacred truce of the white flag, Wild Cat became a most daring enemy to the troops, and kept his warriors inspired to the most savage hostilities.

General Scott was now placed in command of the army, yet the same harassing marches continued, and it was not until seven generals had been defeated at the game of Indian warfare by the wily chieftains that any sign of success was apparent.

Our Government discouraged at being unable to conquer the Indians, or protect the white settlers, again negotiated for peace, but using a more powerful weapon than in former years—that of moral suasion. Executive documents show that all through the war, artifice and bad faith were practiced upon the Indians. The Government was astonished that a few Indians and their Negro allies could defy United States troops. All efforts had failed, even to the horrible policy of employing bloodhounds. To-day we shudder at the barbarity of such an act, but official documents show how much the subject was discussed by Congress and war authorities. A schooner was dispatched to Cuba and returned with thirty-five bloodhounds—costing the Government one hundred and fifty dollars apiece. They were speedily put upon the scent of Indian scouting parties,

but proved utterly inefficient. The public believed the
hounds were to trail Indians, but reports show their
use was to capture Negro slaves. The Seminoles were
a species of game to which Cuban hounds were un-
accustomed and they refused to form acquaintance with
the new and strange objects. The Indians had a secret
peculiarly their own of throwing the dogs off the scent,
and the experiment, to close the war thus, proved a
failure and served no other purpose than to reflect dis-
honor on our nation.

Wild Cat, after his escape from prison, was a
terrible and unrelenting foe. Occupying with light
canoes the miry, shallow creeks, and matted breaks
upon their border, he was unapproachable. A flag was
sent him by General Worth, but remembering well another flag which had meant betrayal, capture and
chains, the daring hero fired upon it and refused to
meet the general. In the summer of 1841, General
Worth's command captured the little daughter of Wild
Cat and held her for ransom. The little girl—his only
child—was the idol of the old warrior's heart. On
learning of her capture, Wild Cat relented, and, once
more guarded by the white flag, was conveyed to
General Worth's camp. History gives an interesting
account of the old chief's approach. His little daughter,
on seeing him, ran to meet him, presenting him with
musket balls and powder, which she had in some way
obtained from the soldiers. So much overcome was
the fearless savage on meeting his child that the digni-

fied bearing so carefully practiced by all Indians, gave way to the most tender emotions.

The moral suasion, the humanity of General Worth made a friend of Wild Cat, and he yielded to the stipulations.

The speech of the old chieftain, because it breathes the same sentiment of the Seminoles of to-day, we give below. Addressing General Worth, he said:

"The whites dealt unjustly with me. I came to them when they deceived me. I loved the land I was upon. My body is made of its sands. The great spirit gave me legs to walk over it, eyes to see it, hands to aid myself, a head with which I think. The sun which shines warm and bright brings forth our crops, and the moon brings back spirits of our warriors, our fathers, our wives and our children. The white man comes, he grows pale and sickly; why can we not live in peace? They steal our horses and cattle, cheat us and take our lands. They may shoot us, chain our hands and feet, *but the red man's heart will be free.* I have come to you in peace, and have taken you by the hand, I will sleep in your camp, though your soldiers stand around me thick as pine trees. I am done. When we know each other better, I will say more."

Through the gentleness and the humanity of the "gallant Worth," Wild Cat at this meeting agreed to emigrate with his people. He was permitted to leave the camp for this purpose. By some contradictory order, while on his way to his warriors, he was captured by one of our commands, put in chains and transported to New Orleans.

When General Worth learned of this violation of his pledge, he felt the honor of our country had again been betrayed, and acting on his own discretion sent a trusty officer to New Orleans for the return of Wild Cat. General Worth by this act, not only showed the nobility of his own character, but proved that the savage heart can be touched with kindness and is always keenly alive to honor and faithful pledges. Moreover the justice of the act had much to do with the successful turning of the war.

When the ship, which brought the chief, reached Tampa, General Worth was there to meet it and publicly apologized to the brave old warrior for the mistake that had been made. Our gallant commander had proven his humane heart, although at expense of both time and money. Through the policy of General Worth, the whole character of the war was changed. On the 31st of July, 1841, Wild Cat's entire band was encamped at Tampa, ready to be transported to their new homes.

The original idea of re-enslaving the fugitives was abandoned. General Worth and Wild Cat now became the most ardent friends—the general consulting with the famous chieftain until every arrangement for the removal was perfected. Seeing a chief of such prominence yield to emigration, band after band gave up the fight and joined their friends at Tampa. From

the time of Wild Cat's removal in the fall of 1841,
until August, 1843, small bands of Indians continued
to emigrate. General Worth now advised the with-
drawal of the troops. A few small bands throughout
the State refused to move, signed terms of peace, however, by which they were to confine themselves "to the
southern portion of the Peninsula and abstain from all
acts of aggression upon their white neighbors." As
vessel after vessel anchored in Tampa Bay to carry
these wronged and persecuted people to their distant
homes, the cruelty of the undertaking was apparent to
the most callous heart. With lingering looks the Seminoles saw the loved scenes of their childhood fade away.
The wails and anguish of those heart-broken people,
as the ships left the shores, touched the hearts of the
most hardened sailor. They were leaving the graves
of their fathers, their happy hunting grounds, beautiful flowery Florida. But it is the destiny of the Indian.
Among that band there was not one voluntary exile.
Poets and artists picture the gloom, the breaking hearts
of the French leaving Acadia; at a later day the same
sad scenes were witnessed on the Florida coast, but
it was not until years after, that a philanthropist gave
to the world an intimation of the melancholy picture of
these poor struggling, long hunted Seminoles leaving
the shores of their native lands.

Part Second

The Present Condition and Attitude of the Seminoles.

TO-DAY, the Seminoles of Florida are a beggared and spectral type of a once powerful race. Secure in the mysterious marshes, they present an eloquent picture of a helpless wandering tribe.

At the close of the war a few bands of the Indians refused to submit to banishment, and concealing themselves in the fastnesses of the everglades, made their removal an impossibility. This part of the tribe, according to their traditions, belonged originally to the Aztec race, and for this reason they claim a pre-eminence over all the tribes of Aborigines of America.

Though defeated in war they never submitted to the Government of the United States, and hence regarded themselves as stronger in character, more valiant in defense, and more determined in purpose than that part of the tribe which succumbed to emigration to the Indian territory. An inexorable decree has forced the Florida Indian into the most desolate lands of the State. Where they once trod as masters they now fear to place foot. We cannot be unmoved by the thought that here are the tattered and poverty stricken handfuls of a tribe of warriors that held at bay a strong government for half a century—a tribe that counted their cattle, their lands and their slaves in magnificent proportions. At the present time, to avoid complications with the South Florida cattle herders, none of the race are permitted to own cattle. There is a certain pathos in the Indian's story of his relation to the white race, which arrests our attention and compels sympathy. But, it is destiny! What of the future? Touch any point in the red man's history, where you will, or how you will, and the helpless savage always gets the worst of it. We judge the Indian too harshly. It is hard to give up old traditions, especially if the adherence to them means a life of ease. We are all in the pursuit of that which will make us happy.

The story is the old one of the merciless extinction of the lower race before the higher. It is a story of the "survival of the fittest." The Florida Indian can go no further. An old anecdote is brought to light which illustrates the Indian's own view of the case. The famous Seneca chief, Red Jacket, once met a government agent, and after pleasant greetings, they both sat down on a log, when Red Jacket asked the agent to "move along." The agent did so and the chief followed. This was done several times, the agent humoring the whim of the old chief, until he had reached the end of the log, when the same re-

quest—"move along," was repeated. "Why man,"
angrily replied the agent. "I can't move along further
without getting off the log into the mud." "Ugh!
Just so white man want Indian to move along—move
along; can't go no further, yet he say move along."
And so with the Seminole to-day. The clearings they
have made in the forests, and the only homes they have
ever known have been bought from the State by spec-
ulators and they are compelled to "move along." The
history of the western Indian as he sells or surrenders
the heart of his great reservation proves that the white
man will have his way. The broken treaties of the
past the Seminole has not forgotten. The old chiefs
are as proud as the most imperious king. They regard these lands as their own, and cannot understand
the government's claim. They say, "what right has
the big white chief at Washington to give to us what
is already ours—the lands of our fathers?" The white
man who receives any confidence from the Florida
Indian, must indeed possess great magnetism, for the
Seminole is suspicious of every overture and will mislead his questioner on all occasions. And while the
white man is studying "poor Lo," "poor Lo" is similarly
engaged in studying him, and continually revolving
in his suspicious mind, "what can the pale face want
from the Indian any way?"

The chiefs have taught the young braves all about
the outrages perpetrated upon their tribe by unscrup-
ulous agents during the wars; and while the Indians

themselves, in many cases practiced cruelty, it was
always in retaliation for some grievous wrong of anterior
date.   History records case after case of robberies and
enormities committed on the Seminoles previous to the
war and during its progress. Micanopy requested a
lawyer to draw a form of writing for him which soon
after proved to be a conveyance of a valuable tract of
land!!! Afterwards the war whoop and the deadly
hand of Micanopy was heard and felt among the
swamps and prairies.

In the mutual relations between the whites and
the Indians, it requires no skilled advocate to show on
which side must lie the wrongs unrepaired and unavenged. Without doubt the Indian has always been
the victim. One thing is certain, the Indian chiefs,
when fairly dealt with, have always evinced an earnest
desire to make just terms. Ever since the Caucasian
landed on the shores of America, a white man with a
gun has been watching the Indian. Four centuries
have gone and with them a record of broken treaties and
violated pledges. The records of the Indian Bureau
support the statement, that before the first half of the
present century had passed, we had broken seven solemn
treaties with the Creeks, eleven with the Cherokees;
the Chickasaws and Choctaws suffered too, saying
nothing of smaller tribes. History reveals how well
the Delawares fought for us in the revolutionary war.
They were brave "allies," fighting out of loyalty to
the "Alliance," and inspired by the promised reward,

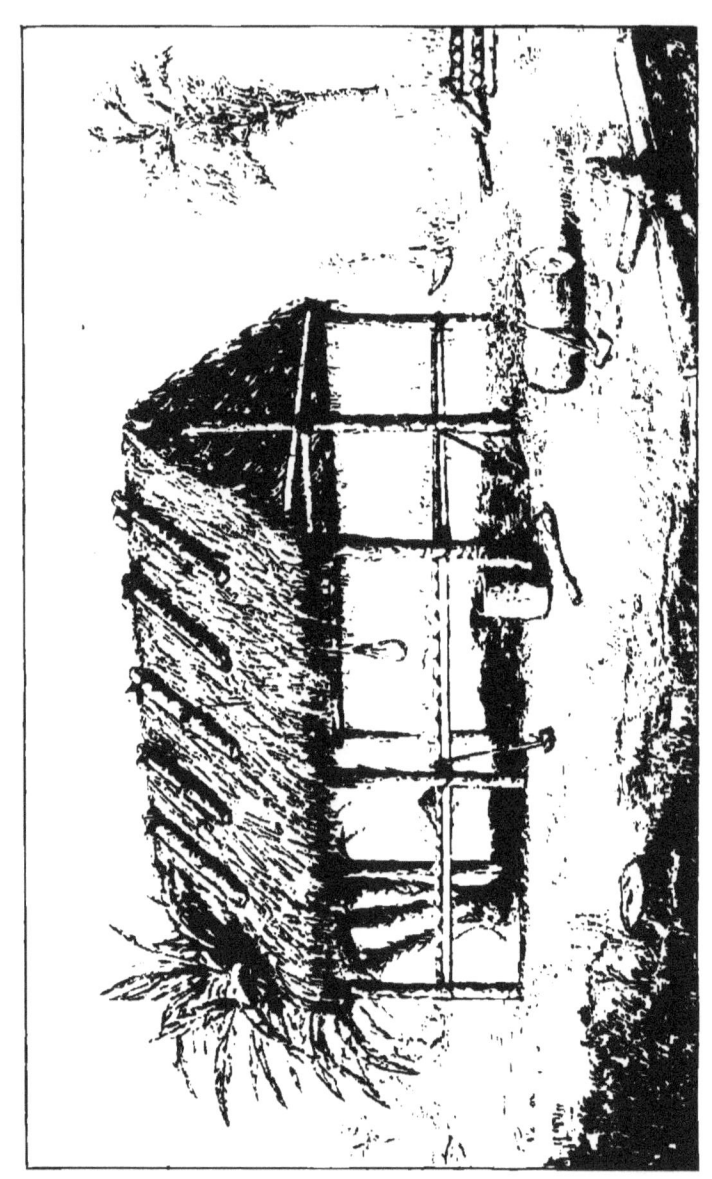

A Seminole Dwelling. (By the courtesy of the American Bureau of Ethnology.)

viz: The "territorial right to a State as large as Pennsylvania and a right to representation in our Congress." But where are the Delawares to-day? One remove after another was made until we find only a remnant existing—some with the Cherokees, and a few with the Wichita agency.

A great deal has been written about the Florida Indian which is not in accordance with facts. There are many obstacles in the way of an intimate acquaintance with their customs and home life. Living as they do in the almost inaccessible morasses, their contact with civilization has been regulated by their own volition. Visitors, traders and government agents have been denied their confidence, and it is only on their visits to settlements for the purpose of trading that they meet the white man. At such times the Seminole is on the alert, ever suspicious, and to the numerous interrogations applied to him by the inquisitive stranger, his answer is an indifferent—"me don't know."

The Seminoles live to themselves, shun all intimacy with the Caucasian, and their personal appearance is therefore almost unknown to Americans. The greater part of the tribe seldom, if ever, leave their marshy homes. To reach their camps uninhabitable wilds must be traversed and sometimes miles of mud and water waded, then, perhaps, only to find the camp deserted. For, while the Seminole has regular settlements, at various times during the year the entire camp will assemble at some point where game is

abundant and a "big hunt" will occupy a few weeks.
Again syrup boiling will be the festival all will join in;
at another time a large quantity of Koonti (wild cassava)
will be made into flour. At these gatherings the tribe
or families occupy temporary dwellings called lodges.

The innate dislike of the Seminole towards strangers
is his hardest prejudice to overcome ; yet he is hospitable
when he convinces himself that the visitor is no government agent, nor comes for any mercenary motive. The
person who is fortunate enough to reach their hunting
grounds, secure their confidence, observe their weird
home life and their childish untutored ways, meets with
an attractive spectacle of romance and may study these
aborigines in their primeval customs. For to-day, with
the exception of the chiefs and a few of the adventure-
some warriors, they know nothing of the innovations
of the last half century. So strong are they in their
resolution to hold no intercourse with our nation, that
neither bribery nor cajolery will have any effect upon
them. A few years ago an effort was made by the
authorities of the Sub-Tropical Exposition at Jacksonville, Florida, to secure a few of the Seminole braves
for exhibition. After many proffered bribes, the young
warriors with the adventurous spirit of youth consented
to go to the " big city." A council was held and the
chiefs said " halwuk (it is bad) : if you go you never
come back." The council of the chiefs is always
respected and the young braves remained with their
fathers. The Indians in Florida number about 600.

They live in tribes apart, each independent of the other, but in friendly relation.

The life of the Seminole has been without any aid or instruction from the white man. He has adopted a few of the implements, weapons and utensils of civilization ; but in no other way has he imitated his pale faced brother. In the natural course of evolution he has made some progress—he has not degenerated.

Government reports show an annual appropriation of almost $7,000,000 for the Indian service; yet the Florida Indian has not received any part of it, and without it he has shown a prosperous condition. The Smithsonian report, in comparing this interesting people with the native white settlers, says, "that success in agriculture and domestic industries is not to be attributed wholly to the favorable character of the climate and soil ; for, surrounded by the same conditions, many white men are lazy and improvident, while the Seminoles are industrious and frugal."

President Cleveland in his message for 1895 pertinently says, " In these days, when white agriculturists and stock raisers of experience and intelligence find their lot a hard one, we ought not to expect Indians to support themselves on lands usually allotted to them." Yet in Florida, we find the red race not only self-sustaining, but refusing any aid from our Government. Several years ago, the Government appropriated $6,000, "to enable the Seminoles of Florida to obtain homesteads upon the public lands, and to establish

themselves thereon." A few of the Indians consented to accept; but the agent, on investigation,
found that the lands which the Indians desired
had passed into State or Improvement Companies.
To-day the Seminole is embittered; and, having
been driven from one reservation to another, he
refuses to exchange "Indian's good lands for white
man's bad lands," and in the bitterness of his conquered
spirit, takes his dusky tribe to the dark shadows of the
cypress swamps, where no pale faced government
officer dare disturb him. Again Congress tacked an
item to the appropriation act giving $6,000 "for the
support of the Seminoles of Florida, for the erection
and furnishing of a school, for teachers and the furnishing of seeds and implements for agricultural
purposes." In the winter of 1889, an agent inspired
with confidence in himself, and with the hope of
manipulating a $12,000 appropriation, came to Florida
by appointment from Washington to renew the effort,
"to find suitable lands upon which to settle the Indians,
and to furnish the seat of an educational establishment."
Securing an interpreter the agent visited the Indian
camp. A council of chiefs listened quietly to his
overtures, but with the same proud spirit of Osceola's
day, they refused firmly to accept any aid from a
Government which they regard as having stolen from
them the lands of their fathers. As the agent dwelt
on the presents the red men of Florida should receive
from the big white chief, Tiger Tail, a worthy de-

A Florida Group.

scendant of the invulnerable Tustenuggee replied, "You
came from Great Chief?   You say Great Chief give
Indian plow, wagon, hoe?" then pointing in the
direction of a small settlement of shiftless whites, he
added, "he poor man, give 'em to him.   Indian no
want 'em."   Delivering his speech with the spirit of
an old Norse king the chief strode majestically away,
leaving the agent no nearer the fulfillment of his trust.
At present, however, there is an Indian agency in
Florida which was established in May, 1892.   The
agency is located East of Fort Myers, and about 35
miles from the nearest Indian camp, and is supported
by a yearly appropriation of $6,000.   The appropri-
ation act reads, "for the support, civilization and
instruction of the Seminole Indians in Florida, $6,000,
one half of which sum may be expended in the
discretion of the Secretary of the Interior in procuring
permanent homes for said Indians."   Little progress
so far has been made.   Five years ago the Government
built a saw mill, and attempted a school, but the Indians,
according to the statement of Col. C. C. Duncan, U. S.
Indian Inspector, to a *Times-Union* reporter, refuse to
send their children to the school or to work the saw
mill.   Many white traders who purchase hides, plumes
and furs from the Indians, tell them that the establishment of an agency is for the purpose of rounding them
up and sending them West.   These Indians have been
cheated and baffled so often by knaves, who go among
them for that purpose, that they imagine all whites to

be of the same character, and cannot tell whether a "talk" comes from their great father at Washington, or whether some impostor be imposing upon them for his own gains; hence the Seminole never removes his cloak of suspicion.

The Government has recently purchased four sections of land, in a cypress swamp about seventy-five miles from Fort Myers, for these Indians. The price paid for said lands is $2,600.

President Cleveland in his message on the Indian question wisely and humanely says, "I am convinced that the proper solution of the Indian problem and the success of every step taken in that direction depend to a very large extent upon the intelligence and honesty of the reservation agents and on the interest they have in their work. An agent fitted for his place can do much towards preparing the Indians for citizenship, and his advice as to any matter concerning their welfare will not mislead." An appropriation of $6,000 may seem small for an Indian agency, yet properly expended good results should follow. The Seminoles are prosperous and industrious, and, aside from providing them with suitable lands, they need nothing more than civilizing Christian influence. Work in this direction has been undertaken and a part of this Florida field is now being occupied, for the first time, by a mission under the auspices of the Episcopal church. While the results so far accomplished are not what might be wished, yet they are of an encouraging nature. The friendship and confidence of the Indians is gradually being secured, which is the chief requisite to the desired results.

We cannot but admire the proud and independent spirit of the Seminole as he refuses, in firm but Indian-like measures, the proffered liberality of a Government which he believes has wronged him. And, from his high pinnacle of pride, he certainly bears the distinction of being the only *American* who has been found unwilling to share the spoils of the nation. So he says, "We have listened to the great father at Washington. The great spirit wishes no change in his red children. If you teach our children the knowledge of the white people, they will cease to be Indians. To know how to read and write is very good for white men, but very bad for red men. Long time ago, some of our fathers wrote upon a little piece of paper without the nation knowing anything about it. When the agent called the Indians together he told them the little paper was a treaty which their brethren had made with the great father at Washington, and lo! they found that their brethren by knowing how to write had sold their lands and the graves of their fathers to the white race. Tell our great father at Washington that we want no schools, neither books, for reading and writing makes very bad Indians. We are satisfied. Let us alone." After this speech delivered in the native tongue, the council breaks up, and the proud Seminole betakes himself to the Everglades. The Seminole is disposed to make a child's bargain with the big white chief. "You let me alone, and I will let you alone."

Photographs of the Carlisle Indian boys have been used to illustrate the improvement which follows education; but the Seminole youth turns away with disdain, as he notes the closely shaven head and the American dress, and says, "Indian no want books, make 'em white man, white man mean heap—lie too much." With a gesture faithful to the Indian, he refers to the "long time ago, Seminoles had lands, cattle, slaves, white man steal 'em." This statement of the Indians is corroborated by the old white settlers of to-day, who fought the Indians. They tell that General Jessup's army, on coming to the great cattle country of South Florida, began a systematic slaughter of all the cattle found. A body of soldiers, too large to fear an attack would round up a herd of the Indian's cattle and sitting on their horses shoot them all down. Up to this time the Indians were regular stock dealers, their customers being the Cubans and the Minorcans. General Jessup's report of his march into the " Indian country " says, "On the 28th (January, 1837,) the army moved forward and occupied a strong position on 'Ta-hop-ka-li-ga' Lake, where *several hundred head of cattle were obtained.*"

The tribe to-day are taught by the chiefs to regard the whites, in general, as lacking in honor and courage, weak and insignificant, or in Seminole dialect, "white man—ho-lo-wa-gus," (no good). This is easily understood when we consider the strong attachment an Indian bears to his native hunting grounds ; and when the memory runs back to the time when our Government banished their friends and relatives to the unknown wilds of the West, and they went silent and weeping towards the setting Sun.   Their bitterness is consistent with their ideas of injustices practiced upon them.

. History, romance and poetry have embodied the characteristics of the red man to our perceptions from childhood.   And while treachery may be a distinguishing feature of the Indian nature, yet the lowest one of them has some conception of honor when fairly approached.   History shows that all through the Seminole war, misrepresentations and dishonorable schemes were practiced against them by the whites. Almost universal sympathy goes out to this remnant of a people who fought so bravely and so persistently for the land of their birth, for their homes, for the burial place of their kindred.   As their traditions tell them of the oppression their people suffered as they wandered in the wilderness thrice forty years, who can tell the secret of their hearts ?   To do this, it would be necessary to become, for the time, an Indian, to put ourselves in his place—and what white man has ever done this?   Ask the waters of Tohopeliga, or the winds that waft across Okeechobee.   To the elements are whispered the heart throbs of these red fawns of the forest. The present Florida Indians are descendants of that

invincible tribe who were never conquered by the force
of arms. Refusing in 1842 to accompany their people
to the mysterious West, they ceased to exist save for
themselves. Finding refuge in the almost inaccessible
Everglades, they were for a time almost lost to the
historian. They have no legal existence, and hence
no rights that a white man is bound, by law, to respect.
There are no Indian troubles in Florida at present, but
every few months a cry comes from hungry land
grabbers, or from trappers and hunters, that the Seminoles are killing off the deer and plume birds. The
changing condition in the lower peninsular country will
eventually lead up to difficulties; and "where shall we
locate the Indians?" becomes a serious problem.

The Florida *Times-Union* editorially says, "All
the murderous, cut-throat, unkempt and squalid Indians
in the United States, whom the Government fears, are
provided with reservations and such luxuries as they
never before had in their lives, but the Seminoles of
Florida, the finest specimens of Indian manhood in
this country, clean in body, pure in morals, and as
brave as the lion that roams the desert, with whom so
many treaties have been wantonly broken, are being
driven farther and farther into the Everglades and their
hunting grounds confiscated to the land grabbers. Is
this justice?"

Should the whites drive off the Seminoles, and
thus approve their greed for land by taking the pos-
sessions the Indians now occupy, what good would it

do them? Internal improvement companies, by their franchises, would sooner or later take the blood-stained acres from them. Let settlers in Florida, or in any part of the country, turn over their accounts and see how many acres have been credited to them, either from the State or from the general Government, without the equivalent of homesteading or for cash. The " Western " style of disposing of the Indian's inherit-ance must not be followed in fair Florida. It seems hard that these natives who ask no aid of our nation, should be forced to the wall by the march of civiliza-tion. To the Western Indians, under the protection of the Government, and supplied in a large measure by the taxes which civilization pays, pages are devoted by philanthropists for the betterment of their condition. The rights of the Seminoles of Florida should be defended. The day is not far distant when they must be made to go to the reservation in Arkansas or to lands set apart for them in Florida. To remove them from their tropical homes to the chilling blasts of the Indian Territory would be an act of cruelty and wholly unnecessary. Those of us who have enjoyed life in this land of the palm, this land of the balmy air and life-giving sunshine, reveled in the eternal bloom of the flowers and the ceaseless song of the birds, can well picture the struggle it would cost the patient Seminole to be forced to a cold western land. No, fair Florida, the ancestors of these proud people were forced to the country of the setting sun silent and dejected. But, with the spirit of Osceola, if they must perish, it will be here—here upon the land of their birth, upon the graves of their kindred. The lands they now occupy are of little value to the white race and might be made a safe reserve for them—forever. Cow boys who hunt upon the Okeechobee plains, say the Indians are peaceably disposed and friendly, and have never yet disturbed or threatened. They are certainly not foot sore for the war path and are fearful of doing any thing to arouse the whites. " Indian no fight," is the answer to the questioner. They have sense enough to know that if war should come again it would mean extermination for them ; and their love for the " Flower Land " is so deep that the thought of exile would cost a struggle they dare not attempt. Yet, feeble remnant as they are, with the same heroic blood coursing their veins that inspired their ancestors and made them almost invulnerable, the present Seminole would choose to die rather than submit to removal. And in their swampy fastnesses, they could maintain a contest that would cost us thousands of dollars and many precious lives.

OUR DUTY TO THESE WARDS OF THE NATION.

Under the present status the Seminoles are prosperous, happy and contented. But the vanguard of civilization is marching on, and thinking friendly minds must solve the question of the protection of this remnant of a tribe we have dispossessed of their natural rights. Dwellers of every land, from Scandinavia to

Japan have a Christian welcome to our shores. The slums of Europe pour in upon us to fill our almshouses and to be supported by our taxes. We have, during the past quarter century, contributed more than $5,000,000 to the education of the freedmen; yet, except in individual cases, the improvement is scarcely noticeable. Men and women are sacrificing their lives for the heathen of other lands.

Christianity is donating millions of money to this end, while our own "wards," too many of them, are yet living in the dark superstitions of their fathers. It is possible it will take time and patience before any shining results are apparent. Not until confidence is restored will the embittered Seminole yield to the overtures of our Government. In an educational sense the older Indians will not be benefitted, except through the influence of their children. The logic of events demands absorption of this people into our National life, not as Indians, but as American citizens; and the sooner they can be induced to accept lands from the Government, and education for the youth, the sooner will the civilization of the Seminole cease to be a theory. The permanent duty of the hour is to prepare the rising generation for the new order of events that must come. Because these bands of the Seminoles are prouder, more invincible than the old Saxons, because they are savages, yet heroes many of them, all the good of life should not be withheld from them. It has taken years of labor to obtain the shining of even the few rays of light that relieve the gloom of the heathen countries of the Orient. It would be unreasonable to expect the offspring of savages to attain in a short time to anything like the thrift of a Nation like ours. Yet, with a few years of humane treatment, unviolated pledges, with Christian and patriotic examples set before them, this little band of Florida Indians would become worthy representatives of this fair land.

Were any future danger to threaten the United States, the Seminoles would be found to be brave allies. The pledge to General Worth by this remnant of hostiles, who in 1842 refused to emigrate with the rest of their tribe, temporarily agreeing "to confine themselves to certain limits and abstain from all aggressions upon their white neighbors," seems to be held sacred by their descendants. Putting the question to Billy Bowlegs, one of the most intelligent of the present Indians, as to what his people would do were the whites to encroach, and take the clearings his tribe are now occupying—"Would Indian fight?" The young brave replied with downcast face, "Indian no fight, Indian no kill, Indian go." Pursuing the subject further—"but Billy, by and by, may be one year, five years, may be, white man go, take all your land, take Okeechobee, then where will Indians go?" With the same bowed head, the answer came low and soft, "me don't know—Indian go." Then to test his idea of an ally the question was asked, "what would Seminole

Indians do, Billy, if the Spaniards from across the big salt water should come to fight the white people of Florida? Quickly and with spirit came the answer, " Indians help white man to fight." Unless action be taken, there will come a time, when, leaving no trace behind him, the Seminole shall pass out of the world— he shall go, like the mist.

We cannot undo the past, but the future is in the hands of the people. In Canada there are over 100,000 Indians. They are called the Indian subjects of Her Majesty; all held amenable to the law and protected by it. Statistics show that on one side of the line the nation has spent millions of money in Indian wars, while on the other, with the same greedy Anglo-Saxon race, not one dollar has been spent, and there has never been a massacre.

The caustic remark that the only good Indian is a dead Indian, might apply to the savage Apache; but when one has studied the home life of the Seminoles, observed their domestic felicity, from which many white men might take example, noted their peaceful, content- ed character, he can only see in them an attractive race, and worthy the proud lineage they claim. Surely if ever the strong were bound to aid the weak, we are bound to help them, to treat them as human beings, possessed of human rights and deserving the protection of American law. This without doubt they will be willing to accept, when our nation by kind, courteous and honorable means secures their lost confidence; and when our national Christianity shall take measures to make our land for them a home where they may dwell in peace and safety.

TALLA-HASSEE.

Almost four hundred years have passed since that fair April day when Ponce de Leon anchored on the verdant shores of Florida. Since the Spanish cavalier planted the silken flag of Spain upon her soil, Florida has been surrounded by a halo of romance and tragedy. Between the time of her discovery and to-day, what marvelous scenes have been witnessed upon her fair plains and along the borders of her wild dark rivers.

The ancient race who greeted the old Castilian has vanished and, save in the little band of Seminoles secreted in the mysterious and weird wilderness of the Everglades, no trace of the red man is visible. A description of a type of this fragment of a people will enable the reader to form a better conception of the tribe as a whole ; and no name is more worthy a place in these pages than that of Talla-hassee.

The old chieftain in appearance is noble and intellectual, and there is that in his look and bearing which at once pronounces him something more than the mere leader of a savage tribe. While his silvered head marks the cycle of many years, in his attire of scarlet and white, embraced by the traditional brightly beaded sash, he exhibits a dignified and patriarchal bearing. His countenance, while indeed mellowed with the cares

Chief Tallahassee.   Martha Tiger.   She yo hee.   Tommy Hill.   Milakee.

of three score years and ten, is kindly and shows a
conquered spirit. The lineaments of noble features
are traceable in the broad forehead, the firm thin lips
and eyes that might pierce the rays of the sun. Talla-
hassee shows no resentment to the whites, yet he believes they have treated the Indian badly.

When Osceola, with his compatriots went on the
war path, Talla-hassee was a small boy and remembers
well when his father and a few companions were surrounded and killed by the soldiers near Talla-hassee,
the capital of the State. Chipco, the chief of the tribe,
was Talla-hassee's uncle; he escaped from the soldiers
and made his way to the Everglades where he lived to
be nearly one hundred years old. Rosa, the sister of
Talla-hassee became his squaw. They were childless,
and at Chipco's death Talla-hassee inherited the title,
but as a reward for bravery displayed in saving his life
on two occasions, Chipco had made him chief years
before he died.

There is no trace of a revengeful spirit in either
word or manner when Talla-hassee speaks of his father's
tragic death, but with the stoicism of a philosopher, he
seems to have accepted it as one of the cruel fortunes
of war, and has nobly "buried the tomahawk." Talla-
hassee is no stern warrior with blood stained hands,
but wears worthily the dignities of his ancestral station
and in many ways might be imitated with profit by his
more cultured pale faced brother. He is a true type of
the "noble red man" and in any other walk of life

would have risen to eminence. Of all the Seminoles, Talla-hassee is the most friendly to the whites. With the inborn courtesy that is native to all true greatness, this untutored Indian will welcome you to his wigwam and with royal grace dispense the hospitalities at his command. Few enter his presence, and none leave it without this mental tribute to his high character. The old chief is treated with care and consideration, and a homage is paid him by the younger members of the band. Among the Seminoles, when a member of the tribe becomes too old for usefulness or self-help, it becomes the duty of the young men to contribute their share to his support. They are taught to do this more as an honor than as a burden.

INCREASING.

It is generally believed that the Seminoles are dying off, and can last but a few years longer. On the contrary, they have large families of strong healthy children, and the past ten years has shown a marked increase in their number. The strict law allowing no persons of a like gens to marry is a reason why the tribe does not multiply still more rapidly. There are instances where eligible young men find great difficulty in getting a wife because of the strictness governing the gens or consanguinity law. One chief has two daughters who find the same trouble in getting married because the men of their choice are too closely connected to them. Thus a member of the Deer clan may not marry into the same clan, no difference how far removed the relationship may be. Relationship on the father's side is not guarded against so strenuously, as the gens is all counted through the mother. Very often the law of marriage causes strange alliances— young men twenty years of age having very old women for wives. From the best obtainable resources, there were in the year 1859 only one hundred and twelve Indians left in Florida. In 1880 by actual count, as reported by the Smithsonian Institute, the Seminoles of Florida numbered two hundred and eight. According to data gotten from the Indians themselves the tribe to-day numbers nearly six hundred. Of this number a great proportion are young children, or in the language of the chief as he made a numerical calculation of the members of the different families—"heap piccaninnies, piccaninnies ojus " (plenty). The Seminoles are divided into four bands, who live in groups apart; each independent of the other, but in friendly relation. They are the Miami Indians, the Big Cypress band, the Talla-hassees and the Okeechobees. Since the death of Woxo-mic-co (Great Chief) five years ago, no one has been elected to fill his place, and it is doubtful if his office will ever be filled.

No event in the history of the Seminole since the closing of the war, has been more tragic than the slaughter of eight of the band, by the hand of Jim Jumper, a half-breed belonging to the tribe. The killing occurred in February, 1891. According to the

Indians, the negro had bought some bad whiskey from a white trader, and it made him "crazy too much in his head"—doubtless delirium tremens. With his Winchester in his hand he started out. The first victim was his faithful squaw who happened to be close by. Rushing forward and through the camp, and meeting the venerable Woxo-mic-co, head chief over all the tribe, who was on a visit to the Cow Creek band from his council lodge at Miami, the crazy half-breed sent a ball through the old chief's head, killing him instantly. Old Tom Tiger, one of the land marks of the Indian wars, hearing the firing came to the rescue, but was shot down before he had time to interpose. Young Tiger, stepping out of the wigwam in time to see his father fall to the ground, with a blood curdling war whoop sprang upon the maniac and a hand-to-hand fight ensued; but he was at the wrong end of the rifle, and before he could wrest it from his antagonist another report was followed by the death cry of the brave young Indian. The wildest panic ensued—the women and children huddling in their wigwams or fleeing to the woods. The murderer now rushed into the wigwam of his sister, and with his knife murdered her and her two little children who were clinging to her dress in terror. Brandishing his knife he started into the woods, where he was killed by a bullet from Billy Martin's rifle. The wailing and the anguish in that camp can better be imagined than described. After the burial ceremony over the murdered victims, the body of the murderer was dragged far into the swamp, to be fed upon by the vultures. Thus passed away in less than half an hour eight innocent lives, victims to the demoralizing influence of the white man's whisky. The Indian village was broken up, the entire band moving away to escape the visitations of the spirits of the murdered ones.

On the death of Woxo-micco, four candidates for the position of Big Chief appeared, but five years have passed and yet no chief has been elected. In the old chieftain's death the last vestige of Seminole war spirit is obliterated. Nowhere in their history is their determination to live at peace with their white neighbors more conclusively proven than in the abolition of the office of Great Chief, "Big Chief" and war councils, in their minds, being inseparable.

The authority of the sub-chiefs, who are leaders of the different bands, is purely personal ; they cannot decree punishment—a jury or council alone can do this. The Government is not harsh, and there is as much freedom as could be possible in these forest homes.

APPEARANCE AND DRESS.

In personal appearance, many a Seminole brave might be taken as a type of physical excellence. He is bright copper in color, is over six feet in height, his carriage is self-reliant, deliberate and strong. His step has all the lightness and elasticity that nature and

practice can combine to produce—as lithe and soft as
the tread of a tiger. The Yale, the Harvard or the
Oxford student with years of training in the athletic
school, would be but a novice in the art of grace,
suppleness and mode of walking, as compared with this
son of the forest. His features are regular, his eyes
jet black and vigilant, always on the alert; his nose is
straight but slightly broadened, his mouth firm as a
stoic's. The hair is cut close to the head, except the
traditional scalp lock of his fathers, which is plaited
and generally concealed under the large turban that
adorns his head.

The dress of the Seminole chief consists of a
tunic embraced by a bright sash, close fitting leggins of
deer skin, which are embellished with delicately cut
thongs of the same material, that hang in graceful
lines from the waist to the ankle where they meet the
moccasin. The moccasin is also made of deer skin
and covers a foot shapely and smaller than that of the
average white man. A picturesque feature of the dress
is the turban. Oriental in its effect, it has become the
emblem of the race. It is worn almost constantly;
and is made impromptu from shawls or colossal handkerchiefs wrapped round and round the head and then
secured in shape by a band, often made of beaten
silver which encircles the whole with brilliant effect.
With young braves the more important the occasion,
the more enormous the turban. Another characteristic
of the dress is the number of handkerchiefs worn,

Billy Buster.   Tommy Hill.   Tallahassee.   Charlie Peacock.

knotted loosely about the neck. Regardless of the temperature, the Indian adorns himself with six, eight or perhaps a dozen of bright bandannas, exhibiting great pride in the number he possesses. A belt made of buckskin completes the costume. From this are suspended a hunting knife, a revolver, a pouch in which is carried the ammunition and small articles necessary for the chase.

The physique of the women will compare favorably with that of the men. They are healthy and robust, and among the younger members some comely well-featured women are found. The dress of the squaw is very simple, consisting of a straight, full skirt, made long enough to hide the feet. The upper part of the dress is a long sleeved, loose fitting waist, which fails to meet the waist band of the skirt by about two inches; this oddly fashioned garment is cut large enough in the neck to be put on or taken off over the head. A large collar, fashioned after the collarettes worn by the fashionables of the season of 1896, completes the toilet. A Seminole woman wears no head dress of any description. Even when visiting the white settlements they go with their heads uncovered. Neither do they wear the moccasins, at home or abroad, in winter or in summer. They are always bare-footed.

Vanity and coquetry are inborn in the female character. The Seminole maiden whose life has been spent among the swamps "far from the madding" crowd and fashion's emporium still practices the arts of her pale faced sister. She affects the bang and the psyche knot with as much ease as the New York belle, and with such metropolitan airs soon captivates her forest lover. The same passionate desire for gold and jewels, ever uppermost in the heart of the civilized white woman, be she peasant or queen, shows itself in the Seminole squaw. Silver breast-plates, made from quarters and half dollars, beaten into various designs add to their personal adornment on festal occasions. What the turban is to the brave, such is the necklace of beads to the woman. It is her chief glory and is worn constantly. Her ambition seems to be to gather as many strings of these brightly colored beads about the neck as she can carry, often burdening herself with several pounds. Even the wee tots are adorned with small strings of the much prized necklace.

A few years ago, chief Talla-hassee with two or three of the squaws visited Kissimmee. Being taken into a room to see a newly born babe, he directed a squaw to take from her neck a string of beads and put it around the neck of the "little white pappoose." This was done as an act of greatest honor, to show the Indian's appreciation of hospitalities received at this house.

INDEPENDENCE AND HONOR.

To-day as we meet the Seminole "at home," we find the wigwam made of palmetto leaves and the skins of wild animals; the floor of this structure is made of

split logs and elevated about two feet above the ground.
A few of the Indians have in late years built board
houses, but the roof is made of palmetto thatch. Here,
surrounded by the gloom and weirdness of the Everglades, miles from white man's habitation, the baying
of the alligator, the hooting of the great horn owl and
the croaking of the heron are the only sounds to be
heard. Truly the picture is one of melancholy and
profound dreariness. But here we find the Aborigines
contented because they are out of the white man's
power. Here they hold their councils, here around the
camp fires the traditions of the old turbaned tribe are
taught to the youths; here too they follow the same
customs of the race of one hundred years ago. Here
is instilled into the youth the story of the perfidies
practiced upon their fathers by the white man; and as
the children listen to the glories of Osceola, and the
tragic ending of their hero, the spirit of conservatism
is engendered, and with swelling hearts they go on, on,
resolute in their determination to avoid disaster, by
keeping aloof from the white man. Although far
from the influence of civilization, knowledge has come
to these people naturally which we have painfully
acquired by books. Driven to these Florida Jungles
after a seven years bloody war, here the Seminole,
thrown absolutely upon his own resources has continued to dwell. He has accepted no aid, his people have
increased, and in a manner have prospered. No almshouses are supported for their benefit. This independ-

ent Indian does not increase the expense of the jail
nor the penitentiary; he is no starving Indian who
must be fed at the expense of the Government. In
these red sons of the forest we meet the original "real
Indian," unchanged by contact with the white man.
The visitor to the "Wild West," who complains that
"the Indians do not look like the Indians of fifty years
ago" would have little ground for his complaint were
he to visit the Seminoles in their marshy fastnesses.
Florida can boast of one of the few tribes of "real
Indians" in the United States. The present Seminole
must be credited with a high sense of honor; and he
can keep a pledge as well as did Massasoit. A few
years ago during a terrific coast storm some Indian braves
asked shelter of a Florida settler. The Indians were
received and entertained until the weather settled. On
leaving, the chief sweeping his hand towards the broad
Savannah, said, "Captian, hunt deer?" The answer
was—"sometimes." "Indian no hunt Captain's deer"
was the rejoinder. Very little in itself, but it meant
much, for since that time there has not been an Indian
hunter within miles of the place.

Famed in song and story is the pledge of the old
turbaned tribe of the Seminoles. Not more worthy
are they of commemoration than their descendants of
to-day. A few months ago, Billy Bowlegs and Tommy
Doctor paid an unexpected visit to Kissimmee. They
walked from their camp at Okeechobee Marsh, a
distance of one hundred and twenty-five miles to tell

Billy Bowlegs.   Tommy Doctor.

their white friend that " Indian no lie." This was all. They apparently had no other business in town, and after a few hours visit left as quietly as they had come. Their mission was completed—their white brother believed them, their honor was clear—they could now dance at the Green Corn Dance with merry hearts.

A few months prior to this, these Indians had promised their white friend to act as guide on a bear hunt in the Everglades. All arrangements had been made for the hunt, except to fix the time and place of meeting. This was to be done through a white settler. Later, plans for the hunt were perfected and word was sent to the Indian village. According to their promise the Indians came to the settler's home on the day specified, but found that the white man had left his house early in the morning with no message as to how or where the Indians should follow. The Indians, not knowing which way to go to find the party, could do nothing but return to their camp—a distance of forty or fifty miles. Subsequent developments proved that the white man wished to act as guide, and thereby earn for himself the remuneration he expected the Indians would receive.

ENDURANCE AND FEASTS.

When one sees the great moral strength of the Seminoles, notes the wonderful physical endurance of which they are capable, observes the fearless, haughty

courage they display, he cannot but be surprised that
the Florida wars were not more disastrous than they
were, or that any of the Seminoles ever yielded to
removal. To test their endurance the old chiefs have
been known to take a live coal from the camp fire,
place it on the wrist and without an emotion let it
burn until the heat was exhausted. Tustenuggee would
remove the cool ember and quietly reach down and put
a fresh one in its place. This old chief, so famous in
history, never yielded to removal and lived till a few
years ago with his tribe in the Everglades. The goal
of the Seminole is to learn to endure and to achieve.
To this end is every Seminole boy educated, and
different modes of developing the powers of endurance
are employed. Carrying a deer for a long distance
without fatigue, walking or running for many miles,
jumping, wrestling, poling a canoe, etc., are some of
the practical modes. The Spartan spirit is supreme in
the minds of the tribe, and the youth are taught that
no merit is greater than that of bearing pain without
complaint. At the annual feast of the Green Corn
Dance the young Indians of a certain age are initiated
into the rights of warriors, and are subjected to trying
ordeals. They must pass through the " In-sha-pit,"
which means the cutting of the legs till the blood
flows, and other cruel arts, after which the Indian boy
is pronounced a warrior, ready for the battle of life,
whatever the Great Spirit decrees. It is the strict
adherence to the teachings of their ancestors that

makes the present generation the brave and proud
people that they are.

Strange as it may seem, the Seminoles celebrate a
Christmas—"all same white man's Kismas" is their
reply when questioned concerning the celebration.
This is the great feast of the "Shot-cay-taw" (Green
Corn Dance), and occurs each year about the first of
July, which is the beginning of the Indian's New Year.
At the annual meeting the whole band assembles for
the feast. The ceremony is largely under the control
of the medicine men who are important personages
among all the bands, and act as advisers, as priests and
as doctors. The medicine men select from the youths
their successors and train them for the position they
must occupy at their death. The Feast, over which
they preside is the fitting time for rejoicing, sorrowing
and purifying. The ceremony preceding the dance
permits all men who have violated the laws to be
reinstated by undergoing certain trying ordeals. The
transgressors appear a short time before the dance.
They are placed in a closed skin tent, where a large
hot stone lies on the fire. The famous " black drink "
of Osceola's time is administered, water is poured on
the stone and the culprits are shut up in this suffocating
steaming heat. If they pass the ordeal they are forgiven
their transgression and allowed to join in the feasting
and dancing when it occurs. The same " black
drink " which is a nauseating medicine, made from
herbs, is taken by all the members of the tribe on the

first day of the dance. This cleanses the system and enables them to "eat, drink and be merry" to the fullest extent. When they are ready for the dance, the shells of the highland terrapin, partly filled with pebbles, are strapped around their legs, and, as they dance, singing the rhythmical long cadenced songs of their fathers, they make melodious music. It is at this time, too, that the fires of the past year are extinguished —not a spark is allowed to remain. New fire is produced artificially ; this is the " Sacred Fire " and must be made with the flint rock of their ancestors. The new fire is presented from one tribe to another and is received as a token of friendship. They then assemble around the fires, singing and dancing. Gratitude is expressed to the Great Spirit if the years have been abundant. If death has overtaken the tribe, mournful strains, expressive of pity and supplication are invoked. This custom was borrowed from the Nachez Indians who worship the Sun. The medicine men arrange the date for the Green Corn Dance, which is governed by a certain phase of the moon, and runners are sent from band to band to announce the time.

At this great re-union old friendships are revived, courtships take a prominent part and plans are formulated for hunting expeditions, syrup boilings and " Koonti gatherings." Members of one settlement will agree to meet certain members of another family, at a certain point and on a fixed day of the moon. There will be no broken pledges—no disappointments.

The Seminole promises nothing to his people that he will not fulfil.

An exciting feature of the dance is the racing for a wife. A level course is laid off and the race begins. The dusky lover selects the maiden for whom he would strive, because he must catch her before he may court her. The Indian girl is his equal, and often his superior in fleetness, and need not be caught unless she so wishes. But, like her civilized sister, she generally encourages the pursuit until she is tired and then gracefully yields on the homeward stretch. However, should she win the race the young lover need have no further aspirations in that direction. He may be saved the embarrassment of future humiliation. One of the most picturesque games enjoyed by the Indians during the Festival is the dancing around the festal pole. On the night of the full moon they dance from sunset until sunrise. It is very interesting to see the harmony in running around the circle as the women throw the ball at the pole in the centre—the men catch it in their bags that are made around a bent stick, which has a bow about four inches in diameter, with a cross on the lower side. When the dancing is over, the circle about the pole is perfectly symmetrical and about ten inches deep, made by the running and dancing.'

SLAVERY.

That slavery exists among the Seminoles is a disputed question. That it does, is known to a few; but

any interference would be received as an act of imper-
tinence by the Indians as well as by the slaves themselves; as was evidenced last winter, when a tourist
meeting Tustenuggee's slave (who was watching the
canoe, while his master sold some skins) attempted to
ask some questions and at the same time to enlighten
the Negro on his true condition. As the chief came
back to the canoe the philanthropic stranger began to
explain his mission. The chief, with the ferocity
which at once stamped him as a true Tustenuggee,
ordered the Negro to "go," which command was instantly obeyed. Then turning to the stranger he said,
"white man's slave free—Injun este lusta (Negro)
belong to Injun—now *you* go." The philanthropist
also quickly obeyed. Talla-hassee's squaw died about
sixteen years ago leaving a family of six boys, the
youngest one being but a small piccaninny. These
boys have been cared for by the two Negro slaves who
speak only the Seminole language and have seemed
perfectly content to do the drudgery for the family.
The number of Negroes among the tribe at the present
time is small. They are allied to the Indians, and
while they are expected to obey, they are treated kindly,
more as companions than as slaves.

Unwritten Laws.

The Government among the Seminoles is peculiar,
it is remarkable, it is magnificent. There is no lying,
no stealing, no murder, and yet apparently there is no

restraining law. Anxiously and carefully have we studied their form of Government, knowing that they leave their money, their trinkets and their garments in the open wigwams. With carefully framed questions we asked of Billy Bowlegs, while on his recent visit to our home, "Billy, your money, you leave it in your wigwam, you go back, money hi-e-pus (gone), Indians steal it, then what you do?" He answered, " me don't know." "Yes, but Billy, white man come in my house, my money steal 'em—by and by, in jail me put him. Indian, all the same, bad Indian steal. What does Indian do?" Again the answer came, "me don't know." Making the points plainer, illustrating by the theft of his gun, his provisions, his moccasins, showing him that a bad Indian from one of the other settlements might come in his absence and steal his winchester, with perfect understanding of our meaning, the reply came as before, "me don't know, Indian no take 'em— Indian no steal." In such a socialistic State, where there is no crime, there can be no punishment. Were a crime to be committed, a council of chiefs would meet and decree a punishment, and it would have enough severity to serve as a lesson for all future miscreants.

The only "fall from grace" we have ever known among any of the bands, extending over a period of ten years acquaintance, was in the case of Buster Flint. Old Buster was a large powerful Indian, but as the braves express it, he was "ho-lo wa-gus" (no good),

"lazy too much," and laid around the settlement as a
regular loafer, too indolent to work or hunt and in con-
sequence was ragged and unkempt. On one occasion
while our tent was pitched near the palmetto wigwams,
and the hunters had been absent for the day, on the
return a small red napkin was found to be missing.
Upon calling Captain Tom Tiger's attention to the fact,
he replied, "me know," and very soon the napkin was
quietly returned to its place. Old Billy could not
resist the bright red cloth and the others knew his
weakness. What punishment was meted to the old
Indian was not learned, but certainly enough to terrify
him during the remainder of our visit.

The Seminoles mean to be honest in their dealings
with the whites. Occasionally the white man may be
deceived when the Indian intends no wrong. As the
National Editorial Excursion made a tour of Florida
last winter, the train made a stop at a little trading
post on the east coast. Quite a joke was innocently
played upon the party by Captain Tom Tiger. A few
Indians had come into the village to trade at the
stores. Captain Tom had brought with him a load of
sour oranges, which grow wild in the region of his
camp. The oranges are beautiful to the eye, but oh,
how bitter! The merry editors saw the golden fruit
and immediately offered to purchase. The chief was
glad to sell, and only asked one cent a piece for the
fruit, but the editors would not take advantage of the
Indian's ignorance of the price of oranges, so they

paid him twenty-five cents per dozen for them. At this
the load of oranges was soon disposed of and the chief,
with perfect honesty of intention in the transaction, was
the proud possessor of about twenty-five dollars. Those
of the party who first tasted the fruit said nothing until all the oranges had been bought; then they were
told to taste their oranges, and a laugh, long and loud
went up from one end of the car to the other, and as
the train rolled away the good natured, but victimized
passengers treated Captain Tom Tiger, chief of the
Seminoles, to a shower of sour oranges. The Indian
was dumbfounded. The wild orange is an article of
barter in Florida, but not until the idea dawn-
ed upon Tom that the excursionists had mis-
taken his fruit for the sweet orange did he awaken
from his bewilderment, and with earnest nods of the
head and impressive gestures he soliloquized, "white
man no like Indian's orange—sour too much. Me tell
white man, one orange, *one* cent. White man tell me
one orange, *two* cents. Indian no cheat white man."

The Seminoles look upon the dim past as a lost
paradise, in which there was happiness and innocence.
" Before the white men came we were men," says the
Indian. Their faith in their forefathers is reverential.
They believe they always did what was right. They
were kind and true to their friends, but terrible to
their enemies.

The Florida Indians are an industrious people.
While the fruits of the chase are their main support,

they cultivate fields, raising vegetables, corn and sugar cane. The men make canoes which they sell to hunters and trappers. Moccasins, baskets and koonti starch, plumes, smoked skins and venison are among their exports. Complaints are sometimes heard that the Indians are killing off the deer and the alligator, which is very true ; but alike are the white man and the negro engaged in the same occupation. Before the white race taught the Indian the monetary value of the game of the country, he slew them only for food and clothing. Long centuries had he lived on this continent, but the herds of buffalo were not lessened ; nor the vast quantities of game driven to the fastnesses of the forest. Till the white trader came to hunt the game as a source of revenue or for ruthless sport, the Indian knew no such motive.

Like his forefathers the Seminole is no prohibitionist, but enjoys the fire water as much as did the savage tribe that drank to Hudson's health. Since that first great tipple in New York, which ended in such a scene of intoxication, causing the Mohicas to name the island " the place of the big drunk," the Indian practices more precaution ; and one of their number always remains sober and watches his boozy brother like a hawk. This is the practice of the Seminoles. Before going on a spree a selection is made of one of their number, whose duty it is to stand guard over all weapons and see that no injury is done to any member of the tribe. The " sprees " in which they indulge are too infrequent to warrant them being classed as intemperate.

Only a few of the tribe talk broken English. The chiefs disapprove of it on general principles—for fear they will talk too much. To keep aloof from the white man, and the white man's ways, is the training of the Seminole youth. Occasionally a few of the tribe leave their marshy homes. These talk English sufficiently to do their trading when visiting towns to dispose of their plumes, deer skins, basket work, etc. These products always find ready sale ; and when the great day of shopping begins a " corner " in red calico and fancy colored beads is the result. The squaws have control of their own money, when on a purchasing expedition, a fact which makes them very *American.*

The squaws are about as social as the half wild deer that are petted by the guests of the St. Augustine hotels. As seen in their camps, clustered together, half alarmed, half curious, the side glances from their dark brown eyes seem to utter a protest against the Government's eternal "move on." A more severely pure minded people are not to be found on the globe. The women are above reproach. Were a white man to insult a Seminole woman by word or look it would be well for that man to never appear in the presence of the tribe again. The Seminole girl who would unwisely bestow her affections would be killed outright by the squaws. In the history of the Everglade Indians only one such case is known, and at the birth of

the half breed child the mother was taken to the woods
and there hung to a tree by the indignant squaws.
The infant was also destroyed. In questioning, as to
which of the squaws did the killing, the answer was
"all, every squaw." On the principle of American
lynch law each hand helped pull the rope.

GENS AND MARRIAGE.

The Seminoles, like other Indian tribes, are classi-
fied by gens. This lineage in the Florida tribe is traced
through the mother. The child belongs to the clan
which the mother represents. The mother exercises
absolute ownership, and should a squaw and her
husband separate for any cause, the children belong
unconditionally to the wife. One young Indian of
our acquaintance is divorced from his squaw. They
have one piccaninny now three years old. Asking the
father to give the boy up, and holding out alluring
inducements, he replied, " Munks-chay (no), squaw's
piccaninny." The gens represented in the Seminole
tribe to-day, are the Otter, the Tiger, the Deer, the
Wind, the Bird, the Snake, the Bear and the Wolf.
Other gens are now extinct in Florida. Thus, in asking
about the Alligator tribe, the chief replied, "all gone—
long time ago—to Indian Territory." A young brave
dare not marry a girl from his own gens, he must select
her from another clan. When asking a chief what
he would do, were he to want a girl from his own gens
for a wife and the girl should want to marry him, he

replied, "Me no marry her." The young Indian is
shy and bashful in his courtships, and having resolved
to marry conceals his first overtures with all the Indian
cunning. His intention is secretly conveyed to the
girl's parents, and should there be no objection the
young woman is at liberty to accept or reject. No
Seminole girl is forced into a marriage. The lover, with
permission to woo, shows some token of affection ; a
deer is killed and laid at the door of the wigwam. If
the present is received the lover is happy. If it remains
untouched, he may do as his white brother does, go
hang himself, or, as is usual, go seek a more willing
fair one. The prospective bride, to show her appreciation of her lover, makes a shirt and presents it to him.
No pomp or ceremony is connected with the marriage.
The day is set by the parents, the groom goes to the
bride's house, at the setting of the sun. He is now
her husband, and at her home he lives for a period.
When the young couple build their own wigwam, they
may build it at the camp of the wife's mother, but not
among the husband's relatives.

BEAUTY AND MUSIC.

The Indian has a high sense of beauty in woman,
as has been demonstrated on several occasions during
their visits to the different towns. A Seminole chief
was taken to the parlor of a hotel, where a new piano
was the exciting theme, to see what effect the music
would have upon his savage mind. But the fair-

haired *performer* absorbed his attention, and with a
shrug which showed his appreciation for beauty more
than for music, he said, " Ugh ! white man's squaw
heap purty."

Music is not a genius with the Seminoles. True,
they have some songs which are monotone and
rhythmical. They are the hunter's songs, the camp
songs and the lullabys. The war songs which sent such
terror to the hearts of the white settlers in Seminole
war days, they seem to have forgotten. Some of the
Indians have natural musical ears, and they are
recognized by their people as musical leaders. They
have no standard pitch, but start their songs where
the natural quality of the voice renders it easiest
to sing. The pitch of the song depends upon the
individual.

An incident, full of pathos, yet illustrating one
of life's parodies, is recalled. It was occasioned by
hearing the music of some old familiar tunes played
in a gruesome Everglade home. As the picture recurs,
one sees a savage tribe—a weird camp scene, with its
storm beaten wigwams in the back ground—and dusky
warriors and squaws moving hither and thither in the
dim shadows of the camp fire. In the centre of the
group sat the musician, who was the happy possessor
of a " box of music,"—an organette which he had
recently purchased. The melodies of " Home, Sweet
Home," " Hail Columbia " and " Nearer My God To
Thee," floated out upon the stillness of the night,

telling the story of the white man's inheritance—
happy homes, a free Government and an ennobling
religion. To the Seminole—God's image in patient
red—the tuneful strains contained no more sentiment
than the murmur of the brook; for they are a people
without a home, without a country, and without a
God in the sense of these songs.

SEMINOLES AT HOME.

A characteristic of the Seminole is to make his
camp in some secreted spot where the white man would
least expect to find his habitation. The peculiar physical formation of Florida makes this very possible. The
Everglade region, which is the immediate environment
of the Seminoles, is a watery prairie, with here and
there high points of ground. On these fertile "hommocks" the Seminole makes his home. Approaching
such a home one sees marks of labor; a clearing is
made, the wigwam is built, sugar cane, corn and sweet
potatoes are growing. A few chickens run around and a
general air of contentment pervades all.

A visit to a Seminole camp reveals many interesting little things which touch the heart and enlist the
sympathy of the observer. The affection displayed by
the stern faced father, when coddling his pappoose, convinces the most skeptical that in the barbarian of the
forest "the heart of man answers to heart as face to
face in water," whatever the skin it beats under. Old
Tom Tiger, without question one of the most ferocious

looking of the Seminoles, would take the baby-boy from its tired mother's arms and softly croon a lullaby, swaying the pappoose backwards and forwards in his great strong arms till the little fellow would fall asleep.

Another instance of parental affection, as given by the Rev. Clay McCauly in his report on the Seminoles of Florida to the Bureau of Ethnology, is full of touching interest. While the incident occurred several years ago, and the little boy is now almost grown to manhood, still it cannot fail to reach the heart of the reader. We give it in the writer's own words. "Talla-hassee's wife had recently died, leaving him with the care of six boys; but the strong Indian had apparently become both mother and father to his children. Especially did he throw a tender care about the little one of his household. I have seen the little fellow clamb-ering, just like many a little pale face, over his father's knees persistently demanding attention, but in no way disturbing the father's amiability or serenity. One night, as I sat by the camp fire of Talla-hassee's lodge, I heard muffled moans from the little palmetto shelter on my right, under which the three smaller boys were bundled up in cotton cloth on deer skins for the night's sleep. Upon the moans followed immediately the frightened cry of the little boy, waking out of bad dreams, and crying for the mother who could not answer; "Its-Ki, Its-Ki, (mother, mother,) begged the little fellow, struggling from under his covering. At once the big Indian grasped his child, hugged him to his breast, pressed the little head to his cheek consoling him all the while with caressing words, whose meaning I felt, though I could not translate them into English, until the boy, wide awake, laughed with his father and was ready to be again rolled up beside his sleeping brothers."

Where the Seminole is hospitable, is around the camp fire and the "Sof-ka" kettle. "Hum-bux-chay" (come eat) is his salutation. The kettle is placed in some convenient part of the camp and at the meal hour the members of the household sit around it. A large Sof-ka spoon rests in the pot and is handed from one to another, each taking a single mouthful. A fastidious taste might shrink from using the large spoon, but to affect such taste would be to offend mine host. Sof-ka is the Seminole standard dish, and is simply a stew made by cooking the meat in a large iron pot, and thickening with meal, grits or vegetables. Sof-ka corresponds in its importance with the Seminole to "frijoles," among Mexicans. The Indians observe a regularity in meal hours, yet at most any hour the Sof-ka kettle is ready for those who may come in from the chase, enhungered. So plentiful is game that it is a common sight to see a saddle of venison or a wild turkey and perhaps a duck roasting before the fire, and, as appetite prompts, any member of the camp may help himself to the savory roast.

The Seminole piccaninnies are healthy, good natured little toddlers, and show no more savage spirit

than do their little pale faced brothers. They play
with bows and arrows, make dolls and play houses,
revel in mud pies, roast the small birds they kill before
a "spit fire," and play they are roasting wild turkey.
They rarely cry, as they are taught from infancy to
show no such weakness; they must obey the slightest
command of their elders. The little four year old is
taught to assist in the duties of the camp. He can
carry water, gather wood, watch the little pappoose,
and learns thus early that he is an important factor in
the tribe.

The boys are allowed to handle no weapons until
old enough to use them successfully. When an Indian
boy is taught to use a winchester and returns from the
chase with his first deer, favors are shown him by the
elders, tokens are presented and he becomes for the
time the young Nimrod of the tribe.

Seminole children are on the whole very much like
other children—some bright, some stupid, some good,
some perverse, all exceedingly human. With the disci-
pline already instilled into their natures, and education,
first for the heart, then for the mind, added, success would
be assured. A Seminole luxury, which serves as a tar-
get as well as a food, is the fruit of the climbing pumpkin vine, which is often seen among the branches of the
trees. When wanted a well directed rifle ball cuts the
stem and the pumpkin drops to the ground. This was
a sport enjoyed by the troops during the Seminole war.

The absence of all earthenware is noticeable in a

Seminole camp. The Seminoles say "long time ago" their race made earthen pots, but white man's kettle "heap good," and they have long since ceased to work in clay. All through Florida pieces of pottery are found in the sand mounds. In the pine forests where the land is good for cultivation, broken pottery is frequently dug up out of the ground. These forests have grown over this land evidently since it was cultivated by former races. The pottery found in parts of Florida, is said by those having made a study of the subject to resemble the Aztec pottery to some extent.

One of the peculiarities of the Seminole man is the number of shirts and handkerchiefs he wears at one time. An instance is related where a white man in company with Billy Ham went out deer hunting. Emerging suddenly from the thick forest, some deer were observed feeding on the Savannah in front of them. The Indian was dressed in the bright colors of his race, and stealthily slipping back into the shadows of the trees, he began to remove shirt after shirt and untie handkerchiefs from around his neck. As each article was removed, the Indian became less conspicuous. After divesting himself of six or eight shirts, and eight or ten handkerchiefs, the Indian and his costume now blended with the surrounding objects. His dusky form was in perfect symphony with the dead leaves and grasses, through which he silently crept towards his prey. The Indian prefers to make sure of his game by creeping upon it. He can advance to

within a few feet of a deer. The deer, while feeding
is always on the alert for an enemy. If it sees nothing
moving it will not be alarmed. This is where the
strategy of the Indian comes in. He stops just before
the animal raises its head. The lifting of the head is
always preceded by a movement of the tail, hence the
cunning Seminole watches the tail, and knows when
to be still.

BILLY BOWLEGS.

A few weeks ago, after many invitations, Cho-
fee-hat-cho (Billy Bowlegs), a warrior of more than
usual intelligence made his long promised visit to
Kissimmee. Here, away from his natural surroundings,
one could study his Indian characteristics from an
unprejudiced stand-point. As a specimen of manhood
he is far above the average. Although six feet two
inches tall, he is so symmetrically proportioned that
one loses sight of his height. His features are good,
his hands and feet remarkably small, his voice soft
and low—a characteristic of every Seminole. His
dress was the holiday attire of his tribe; he wore a
gold watch and chain, and regulated his time-piece
by the railroad clock. To the stranger he was all
indifference, answering "yes," "no," "me don't
know," as it suited him. While his visit extended
over a period of three days, he showed no special
restlessness. At the table he was on the alert and
readily followed the manners of his host. He was
cautious to help himself sparingly until urged to—

"hum-pee-ta tee ti-es chay" (eat plenty). The knife and fork he used with as much ease as if it were a daily practice.

At the ringing of the church bells on Sunday morning, it was explained to the Indian that they were to call the people to the church, so that the minister might tell them of the white man's God. With the inquiry, " You go ? " to his host, receiving an answer in the affirmative, Billy said, " me go too." He was escorted to the chapel, and through the long service was a model of propriety, and conformed perfectly to the customs of the church. He expressed himself later as liking the music, but remarked that the preacher talked too fast.

Such names as Tom Tiger, Doctor Tommy, Wild Cat and Billy Bowlegs, are the white man's names for the Indians. Each Indian has his Indian name, which is significant of some family or personal characteristic, and which contains the root word of the gens to which that Indian belongs. During the Indian's visit, he expressed a wish to have the Seminole names of a number of his people written down so that he might make a copy and carry home with him. Certainly this young brave could not be called stupid or sluggish. Knowing that the information we sought was for the purpose of putting it into a book, so that " the people could read about the good Indians of Florida," he showed the greatest interest in the questions, making his answers direct and truthful. An air of deepest

solemnity would rest upon his face until he was assured
his meaning was thoroughly understood. During his
visit he expressed an eagerness to learn to read and
write, and followed a copy with remarkable exactness.
With the desire to read and write, however, ended all
ambition to be like the white man.

Every effort was made to please so rare a visitor,
favors were shown him, in fact, he was treated as a
most honored guest, yet this son of the forest received
it all with a silent dignity that would have graced a
monarch. When he was ready to leave, he quietly
arose, remarking, " me hi-e-pus " (go), and noiselessly
passed out of the house.

It is a disputed question whether a wild Indian
of pure blood has ever been permanently civilized.
One of the missionaries of the Osage band once said
that " it took fifteen years to get the blanket off
Joseph Pawnee-o-passhee, Chief of the Osage tribe,
and it took Joseph just fifteen minutes to get it on
him again.

RELIGION.

A pretty tradition among the Seminoles is that a
beautiful race of Indians, whose women they call the
daughters of the sun, reside among the swamps and
lakes of the O-kee-fee-no-kee wilderness and live in
un-interrupted felicity upon islands of eternal verdure,
feasting upon the luxuries of the islands, but inaccessible to the approach of human footsteps.

Unlike the child of Africa, who lives in a world

of ghosts and goblins, the Seminole is not superstitious. He has his traditions, his mythologies, and on these are based his history. He obeys the Great Spirit, but it is not from any spirit of fear; it is the teaching of his fathers, and becomes the duty of the Indian. The religion of the Seminole has been without question the most difficult of all their history to reach.

Their conception of the creation of man is very unique. "Long time ago, E-shock-e-tom-isee (God) took seeds and scattered them all around in a rich valley bordering a river. By and by God saw fingers coming out of the ground and great people—heap too many came up from out of the sand. Some went to the river and washed, washed, washed too much; it made them weak and pale; this was the es-ta-chat-tee (white race). Others went to the river and washed not too much, they returned full of courage, strong heap; this was the es-ta-had-kee (red race). The remainder no wash, lazy too much, es-ta-lus-tee (black man)."

In an extract taken from an old history printed in London in 1776, descriptive of the native inhabitants of Florida, these people are described as idolaters, worshipping the sun and moon—the worship consisting of saluting the rising sun, chanting to his praise and offering sacrifices to the planet four times a year. They believe that the sun was the parent of life.

Whatever may have been the ancient rites of this race, the present people seem to have outlived all remembrance of them as well as of their early ancestors themselves. A glimmering of the Christian religon, no doubt instilled into the race more than two hundred years ago by the Franciscan priests, still seems to linger among the descendants of to-day and constitutes their religion largely. These rites they observe as faithfully as they did a century ago; and yet in all that time they have received no further teaching, and have no personal knowledge of the civilizing effects of the gospel of Christ. In the same length of time where would have been the religion of the Caucasian race, without the divine word, and without the influence of men who have devoted their lives to the cause of Christianity? The Seminoles believe in God (E-shock-e-tom-i-see), and that God had a son (E-shock-e-tom-i-see-e-po-chee) who came on earth and lived with the Indians "long time ago, to make them good Indians." Christ, according to their traditions, was killed by the "wicked Spaniards" when they first came to this continent. Since that time it has been the duty of the medicine men to teach the Indians "to think with God," and to impart the Great Spirit's wishes to his red children. Each tribe has two or more medicine men who act as priests as well as doctors. These men are highly honored by the tribe, because they believe them to be directed by the supreme being. Just before the festival of the Green Corn Dance the medicine men leave the tribe, and going to a secret spot, there build a lodge. Here they fast for twenty-four hours, after which they take a potion, made of herbs, which causes a deep sleep to come over them.

It is now that God appears to them in a dream and tells them how to make the Indians "think good," and how they shall prepare the herbs for medicine. Returning in time to prepare for the great feast they occupy a most prominent position in the dance circle. The Seminole tradition of Christ's coming to live with the Indians, is that the son of God just stopped at the most Southern point of Florida, at which place he was met by three Indians who carried him around the Southern Peninsula on their shoulders, while he sowed the seeds of the "Koonti" root which was God's gift to the red men. (This Koonti is a wild cassava and found only in the extreme Southern portion of Florida.) According to the legend the Indians were in a starving condition. The ground was parched, no corn grew and the game had all left. During the long time in which the Indians waited for the Koonti to grow, God rained down bread "heap, plenty," which the Indians gathered and ate. In describing this bread, which came down in the rain each morning, the Indian illustrated in this wise—"Littly bread, white man's biscuit all the same, good, every Indian eat plenty." The Mosaic account of the manna from Heaven is evident in this legend.

The Seminole believes in a future state—In-li-Keta (Heaven or Home). To this place do the good Indians go after death. Here they may "hunt, hunt, hunt, plenty deer, plenty turkey, plenty bear find, and cool water ojus (plenty) all the time. Bad Indians

after big sleep hunt, hunt, hunt, deer, turkey, bear—
no find 'em, hot water drink all the time."

After death the body of a Seminole is immediately
prepared for burial—the corpse being clad in new
clothes. When a chief dies one cheek is painted red,
the other one is painted black. The rest of the tribe
do not have the face painted for burial. It will be recalled that Osceola, with the death struggle already
upon him, rose in his bed, and "with his own hand
painted one-half of his face, his neck and his throat,
his wrists, the back of his hands and the handle of his
knife red, with vermillion"—the marks of a war chief.

At sunrise, on the day following a death, the body
is carried by two Indian men to the place of interment.
The corpse is placed on a base made of logs with the
face to the rising sun. If the deceased be a warrior,
his rifle and accoutrements are placed by his side, "that
he may be fully armed on his arrival at the happy
hunting grounds." A bottle of Sofka is buried with
him that he may eat on his long journey. Around
the body is built a pen of logs sloping till they close at
the top and thickly covered with palmetto leaves.
The protection is to prevent the wild beasts from dis-
poiling. With faces now turned reverentially to the
rising sun, they commend into the keeping of the
Great Spirit the bivouac of the dead. The bearers
of the dead then make a fire at each end of the grave,
and the mourners return to camp, the women loudly
wailing and tearing their hair. At the death of a

husband the widow must live with disheveled hair for one year. Her long black tresses are worn over her face and shoulders, and she presents a forsaken, pitiable appearance. At the end of twelve moons her period of mourning is over and she may again arrange her hair, don her beads, which have been removed during her period of mourning, and may marry again. The husband, on the death of his squaw, may not hunt for four days, and for a period of four moons must appear in mourning, which consists in the removal of his neck handkerchiefs, and the laying aside of his turban. When a death occurs in one band or settlement, the news is not communicated to the other bands until such time as it is convenient for a messenger to be sent.

Bought Back.

About fifteen years ago, one young Indian brave, Ko-nip-hat-cho, by name, stepped beyond the Seminole law and asked permission to live with a white man, at Fort Myers, Florida. He was eagerly received by the gentleman, and was taught much of the English language and civilized mode of living. But for a Seminole to so far forget the teachings of his fathers, as to wish to affiliate with the white race, caused the greatest dissatisfaction in the Indian camps. " Talk after talk " was " made " by the chiefs as they met in council concerning the actions of this bold young Indian. He was repeatedly warned to return to the tribe. They even threatened to kill him if he refused to do so. At length, however, artifice succeeded, where all else had failed. The daughter of Charles Osceola was promised him for a wife if he would but return to his people and once more don the costume of his race. No Indian girl in all the nation could boast of the beauty of Nan-ces-o-wee; damask and dark, with features as refined as the Caucasian, a form superb in its symmetry, a step as graceful as the doe's—a spirit as fearless as the falcon—such is the woman who moved Ko-nip-hat-cho from his foreign alliance. Ko-nip-hat-cho has four children, is contented and happy in his forest home, and with his knowledge is an important personage among his tribe. His wife is the belle of the Seminole nation. All the Indian braves say, " Ko-nip-hat-cho's squaw *heap purty*," and in their native tongue declare, " Nances-o-wee most beautiful of all the Seminole squaws."

MOUNDS.

The great number of mounds found in Florida afford attractive study to the lover of scientific research. These mounds are of many shapes, heights and areas. They are found in all parts of the State, but are more abundant on or near the coast and along the water courses. Every few months some explorer, armed with shovels, picks and other instruments used in excavating mounds, comes before the public and announces new discoveries, based on new theories. The best possible explanation of the source of these

mounds is founded on the theory that they are of
Indian origin. One scientist has aimed a happy
stroke at writers of our antiquities when he says,
" Whoever has time and patience, and will use his
spade and his eyes together, and restrain his imagi-
nation from running riot among mounds, fortifications,
etc., etc., will find very little more than the indications
of rude savages, the ancestors of the present race."
No better theories can be advanced than those of
Major Powell, who says, " remove the Indian element
from the problem and we are left without a hypothesis."
One of the latest mound excavations in Florida was
made by Dr. Moore. A thousand skeletons were
unearthed as well as many articles of pottery, and
other things considered of great value by the explorer.
The height and character of the Florida mounds indicate the different uses for which they were built. These
mounds vary from three feet to thirty feet in height,
and their areas range from a few square feet to four
hundred feet square. The shell mounds which are
numerous throughout the peninsula seem to have
grown without any idea of purpose by the builders,
and are merely accumulations of shells and soil. Year
after year it was the custom of the tribes to congregate
at certain localities for their festivals, and, living on
shell fish, the shells in course of time formed vast
mounds or elevations. There are a number of small
mounds on the outskirts of Kissimmee City. Excavations have been made, and pieces of skeletons, beads,

pottery and gold trinkets were exhumed. Other mounds in Florida indicate that they were built for tombs, while others, being composed of stratas of sand and other soils, from their height might have been built for out-looks or signal towers. Chroniclers of De Soto's day describe the manner in which the natives brought the earth to these spots and formed these elevations. The Indians say in Seminole war days these mounds were used to build their signal fires upon. By smoke telegraphy, they communicated war news from one band to another. By this means, with their fleet Indian runners, who acted also as spies, the entire tribe was kept informed of the innermost workings of the white army. In asking a chief about the burial mounds, he answered, " long time ago heap many people here," and that their " ancestors buried their dead in mounds so that other bands coming along might not disturb their bones." Many times the body would be carried a great distance in order to bury in a sepulchre where rested the bones of their ancestors. " Now," the chief says, "Seminoles no fight, not too many people;" and he buries his dead near his camp.

PICTURE WRITING.

The Seminoles have no picture writing, nor do their minds in any way run to art. They prefer the rough athletics of forest life, which educates them for the chase and makes them the vigorous and hardy people that they are. They would sooner " hook " an alligator than paint the finest picture the brush is capable of producing, and yet there is nothing in the white man's home they enjoy more than studying the pictures of a book. In this way they may be taught much. Through the teaching by pictures they have learned the story of Pocahontas, and of William Penn, "the red man's brother." On an occasion the picture of a heathen Zuni god was shown to an Indian and its meaning explained. The effect produced would have done credit to a Christian believer.

MEDICINE.

The Seminoles have a superstitious faith in the efficacy of certain roots and herbs known to their tribe, the knowledge of which has been handed down from their remote ancestors. The curative property of these plants they never question. A few of the band to-day have carefully concealed about them small pieces of a root, which they call "hil-lis-waw." This root was gotten by some of their tribe sixty years ago when their people were encamped at Tampa, and has been carefully treasured ever since, having been handed down from father to son. Their faith in the healing powers of this root is marvelous, their idea being that the smallest possible piece being made into a tea would restore life from death almost. Those fortunate enough to own a small piece the size of a pea are considered to have a great treasure. On testing this root it was found to be a simple plant, the great medicinal

qualities of which exist largely in the minds of the
Indians. They are ignorant as to what the root is and
believe it to be very valuable, saying, "so much,"
(what one could hold in the palm of the hand) "cost
$25." "Long time ago," says the Seminole, "chief
sick *heap* too much; by and by, big sleep come.
Medicine man bring hil-lis-waw, fix 'um, quick. Chief
get well."

Pais-haw is the name applied to a plant which the
Indians regard as an antidote to the rattlesnake bite.
Old settlers tell that they have known of Indians
allowing themselves to be bitten by a rattler on a
wager of a silver dollar. The Indian after being bitten
would go to the woods, a short distance away, and procure their antidote. Returning they would apparently
be no worse for the bite. Requesting an Indian to
procure some of the roots, he replied, "No find 'em
here—by and by me go to Okeechobee swamps, find
'em plenty."

A few weeks later there came through the mail a
small box full of roots, neatly done up and addressed
by the Indian's own hand, a perfect copy of name and
address as he had learned to write it during his visit.

On sending the roots to the Smithsonian Institu-
tion for analysis, the secretary reports that they belong
to a species of plant known as *Cyperus*, and adds,
"This is one of the large number of reputed cures for
snake-bites, which have become so regarded from the
fact that a person who has been bitten has been known

Billy Ham.   Charlie Peacock.

to recover after taking the drug." The use of water
enters largely into the materia medica of the Seminoles, bathing in cold water being one of their principal treatments for fevers. During the war with the
whites a soldiers' camp was found deserted; the Indians
immediately appropriated the clothing, blankets and
other things. Very soon the loathsome disease of
small-pox broke out among them. Ignorant as to the
nature of the malady, they immediately applied their
bathing remedy. The result was a frightful mortality,
few of that band were left to tell the story. In this
instance the Government Army gained a victory over
their foe without the firing of a gun.

ABIDING WORDS OF BEAUTY.

All through Florida the musical softness, peculiar
to the Seminole dialect, is sustained in the names of the
lakes and rivers. Each having a history descriptive of
its character, or some incident connected therewith.

The old names of the chiefs were very euphonious,
such as Osceola, Micanopee Tusteenuggee, Coacoochee
and Talla-hassee. These are being displaced by names
adopted by the whites, such as Billy Ham, Tommy
John and Billy Buster. Accident, too, seems to have
credited the Aboriginese with words not really their
own if it be true that "Yankee" is only the attempt
made by the Indian to speak the word English, and that
pappoose is the effort of the natives to say "baby."
The symphonious cadence of such words as Alabama,

Tuscaloosa, Caloosahatchee and Minnehaha has often been noticed.

Tohope Ke-liga is the name of one of the most beautiful lakes in Florida, its Indian significance meaning "fort site." All around the lake are the old hunting grounds of the Indians and memorable points in Seminole war fame. To-day the Okeechobee drainage canal connects it with the lakes south, plantations surrounding its shores; the thriving city of Kissimmee is situated on its North side and all trace of the Seminole has vanished. The only memorials he has left are his words firmly embedded in the history of his conquerors. Kissimmee river is said to have taken its name from a romantic episode. A young Spanish grandee in a moment of impulse snatched a kiss from a Seminole girl, and the frightened maiden's child-like plaint to her mother established the name of the river on whose banks the kiss was stolen—Kiss-him-mee. We-la-ka is the Indian name for the St. John's river and describes it so graphically that the old Spaniards retrograded when they named the "river of lakes," for their patron saint. Ock-la-wa-ha, "crooked water," appropriately describes the most crooked stream in America. Okeechobee, with her vast expanse of water and over-hanging mists, in Seminole significance means "the place of big water." With la coochee, so memorable in Seminole war days as the place of Osceola's strategic movements, is a long but very narrow stream meaning in the Seminole tongue "Little

Big river." Alachua—"the big jug without a bottom," We-Kiva—"mystery," and so on all over the peninsula do we find names preserved which mark the wanderings of the picturesque Aborigines.

In dealing with the Seminole language we meet with long words and mammoth expressions. The Seminole greeting, "Ha-tee-eten-chee-hick-cha-hit-is-chay sounds formidable, yet it only means "glad to see you." These, with well understood Indian phrases such as "burying the tomahawk," "going on the war path" we employ familiarly without a thought of the tribe we have dispossessed. The time for studying the Aborigines of America will soon be over. Only remnants of tribes remain among us. Old myths and customs are being displaced by new ones, and we can truly see that the red man's inheritance is nearing the horizon of its destiny.

CONCLUSION.

When the "last Seminole" goes, he will in every sense be the "last." He will leave no history; neither monument. His narrow path through the Savannah lasts no longer than the doe's road to the ford of the stream. His race have had their joys, their triumphs and their defeats, and then been swept into oblivion. As memories come up, we hear the faint rustle of the leaves and see the dusky forms of these ancient people as they glided through the leaf carpeted aisles of the forests.

Thou, Florida with thy laughing waters and sunny skies, art the Seminole's elysium. Thy spreading palms form the only canopy he desires. To part from thy loved scenes would be like separating from his kindred. No, under the shadows of the live oak and the magnolia has he lived, under their shadows let him die.

As the patient Seminole, with swelling heart "moves a little farther, and yet a little farther," he goes not willingly, but with a sad heart and a slow step. Micanopy, when told by the officers, that he might choose between emigration and death, answered, "Kill me here then—kill me quickly." The same spirit is manifested by the Seminole to-day when he says, "We have never done anything to disgrace the land of our birth, nor the honor of an Indian. For fifty years the pledge to our great father has been kept inviolate. Our tongues are not forked and our feet tread not in the white man's path. We threw away the rifle and grasped hands with the white skin. We know the white man's power, and though we love peace, we fear not death. We will not leave the land of our birth. The Great Spirit loves his red children, and says to them, 'your bones must rest with the dust of your fathers.' Brothers, when the pale face came to the shores of our land, our fathers made him a fire from their flint rock to warm by, and gave him hominy to stay his hunger. Brothers, the Seminole wishes no harm to the white race, but his heart heaves and

surges as it says, 'let us alone—let us alone' Though
you slay us, you shall not move us."

"A kingdom as full of people as hives are of bees,"
wrote the first discoverer to King Ferdinand. Where
are they now? As the stars and stripes proudly herald
liberty and independence to the corners of all Nations,
how can we be unmindful of that "charity which
begins at home?" The panorama of Indian history
passes before us, and we see nothing more tragical than
the pictures of the wrongs endured by the native population. Let us then deal kindly with the tribes we
have dispossessed, whose removal to the swamps has
made room for our own enlargement. In the persons
of these descendants of a now disinherited race, who
with shy, frightened faces still hide in the wilderness,
we may yet atone in part for the tragedies of the past,
by making Florida a free, safe and Christian home for
this patient, and long persecuted remnant of a once
powerful Indian Nation.

Introduction to Vocabulary.

I N PRESENTING the following words, phrases and
sentences to the public, we beg to add a few ex-
planations. The words have been obtained from
the Indians themselves. To collect words from an Indian requires patience at any time, and in dealing with
the Seminoles particularly so. The Florida Indian is
suspicious of the white man, and until a confidence
was established and a friendship formed, it was impossi-
ble to obtain any accuracy from him. To secure the
words in this work methods were devised, in order to
have the Seminole fully understand the collector,
as well as to enable the collector to grasp with a
certainty the Indian's meaning. As will be seen by
a close study of the vocabulary, the noun does more
than simply denote the thing to which it belongs—
it also assigns to it some quality or characteristic.
As for instance the word elephant. The Indian
had never seen an elephant, but on being shown
one in a circus parade, after a careful thinking, he
named it, " e-po-lo-wa-kee " — "heap long nose."
Great latitude is thus permitted in an Indian vocabu-

lary.   On account of non-intercourse with a civilized
race the Seminole language is very pure.   Economy in
speech is followed, the highest aim of the Indian being
to express in a single word both action and object.
Every cluster-word is a description—or a definition.
The study of an unwritten language finds its phonol-
ogy difficult.   In this collection, the words are spelled
phonetically; the accent and division into syllables are
indicated to assist the student to make the correct pro-
nunciation.   Not only were these words given in good
faith by the Indians with the present use in view, but
each succeeding year, as we visited the Glades for a
hunt, the various members of the tribe showed decided
interest in our note book—assisting in revising the
words by going over and over again the Seminole
meaning and accent.   The Seminole has a keen sense
of humor.   As we gathered words and phrases many
amusing incidents occurred, always at our expense and
to the greatest merriment of the Indians.

    To Talla-hassee are we indebted for much of this
vocabulary, as well as for many interesting incidents
and fragments of the history; yet it was not until the
fourth year of acquaintance that the old chief, beside
the dying embers of our camp fire, at the midnight
hour opened his heart and told the story of his people,
their myths, religion, legends—their heartaches.   The
night was chilly, the old chief lost in his own earnest-
ness drew his tunic closer about him, yet the writer
could not say "it is late—you are cold."   It was a

golden opportunity a word, the rustle of a branch and the current would have changed. Until daybreak, in his broken English Talla-hassee told his story. Never before, nor ever since has such an occasion presented itself.

J. M. WILLSON, Jr.

Kissimmee, Florida.

Vocabulary.*

Persons.

SEMINOLE.	ENGLISH.
Es-ta-chat-tee	Indian.
Es-ta-had-kee	White man.
Es-ta-lus-tee	Negro.
Ho-non-waw	Man.
Hoke-tee	Woman.
Ach-o-be-li-tee	Old man.
Hoke-tee-li-tee	Old woman.
Ho-non-wa-mi-nit-ti-tee	Young man.
Hoke-tee-ti-mi-nit-ti-tee	Young woman.
Che-pon-no-shi-tee	Boy.
Hoke-ti-chee	Girl.
Est-to-chee	Infant.
Ho-non-o-chee	Male infant.
Hoke-to-chee	Female infant.
Poke-taw	Twins.
E-hi-wa-o-chit-ee	Married man.
E-hi-was-ko	Bachelor.
E-hi-wa-se-ko	Widower.
E-hi-lift-mus-chee	Widow.
E-he-see-ko	Old maid.
E-he-see-ko-hoke-ti-lee	The old people.
Es-tee-min-nit-tee	A great talker.
O-pa-na-ki-tee	A silent person.
Host-cope-e-taw	Thief.
Host-cope-e-gost-chee	Not a thief.

* In this vocabulary the words are arranged according to their subject or character, no attention being paid to alphabetical succession.

Parts of the Body.

SEMINOLE.	ENGLISH.
E-caw	Head.
E-caw-e-see	Hair.
E-caw-hos-pee.	Crown of head.
To-so-faw	Face.
Ka-ho-waw.	Forehead.
E-tox-lo-waw	Eye.
Tose-lis-kee	Eye lash.
To-do-no-lup-pa-is-see.	Eye brow.
Tode-le-wa-hos-pee	Upper eyelid.
Tode-le-list-la-hos-pee	Lower eyelid,
Hots-cote-es-caw	Ear lobe.
E-hots-ko	Ear.
Hots-caw-pof-ef-caw	Perforation in ear.
Hots-caw-ko-kee	Opening of ear.
E-ho-po	Nose.
E-po-fo-nee	Ridge of nose.
E-po-haw-kee	Nostril.
E-yan-i-waw	Cheek.
No-ti-ka-is-see	Beard.
E-choke-o-waw	Mouth.
Choke-hos pon-a-paw	Upper lip.
Choke-hos-pee	Lower lip.
E-no-tee-ho-maw	Front teeth.
E-no-tee-lock-ko	Back teeth.
To-los-waw	Tongue.
E-to-ka-lo-swaw	Saliva.
Sin-no-ka-nil-caw	Throat.
No-ti-caw	Chin.
No-ka-pee	Neck.
No-quif-pa-tock-ock-naw	Adam's apple.
E-naw-chee	Body.
E-faw-chaw	Shoulder.
Fo-lo-taw-pix-taw	Shoulder blade.
E-claw	Back.
E-claw-fo-nee	Back bone.
E-hoke-pee	Breast of man.

SEMINOLE.	ENGLISH.
E-pee-sec	Breast of woman.
Im-po-loke-cho	Hip.
E-ho-cho-waw	Navel.
E-shock-paw	Arm.
In-clop-pe-claw	Right arm.
Aw-clos-clin-aw	Left arm.
Ho-lo-wa-to-tce-ta-gaw	Arm pits.
Sock-pof-o-nee	Right arm above elbow.
Aw-kos-ko-nof-o-nee	Left arm above elbow.
E-ko-chee	Elbow.
In-tee-ti-pix-tee-e-toke-kee-ta-gaw	Wrist.
In-tee-ti-pix-tee	Hand.
In-ko-faw	Palm of hand.
In-tee-ta-pix-tee-e-naw-pa	Back of hand.
In-ka-we-sa-kaw	Fingers.
Som-kit-kee	Thumb.
Som-kil-smil-kaw	First finger.
In-ka-nock-klo-pa-ho-e-claw	Second finger.
In-ka-ho-klif-claw-such-lo	Third finger.
In-ka-its-ho-chee-wa-chee	Small finger.
In-hits-kee-in-kose-es-waw	Finger nail.
In-ka-we-sock-ka-e-to-pee	Knuckle.
In-ka-yock-pee	Space between knuckles.
E-tol-kay	Rump.
Chee-hof-ee	Leg above knee.
E-tolk-wa-po-la-ko	Knee.
Tose-to-po-la-ko	Knee pan.
Chee-host-go-waw	Leg below knee.
E-lim-pock-ko	Calf of leg.
E-lay-toke-to-swaw	Ankle.
E-lit-ta-pix-tee-e-fo-cho-to-kee-not-ee	Instep.
Es-tel-e-po	Foot.
Es-tel-e-ho-faw	Sole of foot.
E-lich-es-caw	Heel.
Es-tel-e-e-sa-caw	Toe.
Es-tel-e-eeds-kee	Large toe.
Es-tel-e-nock-clay-ho-e-claw	Second toe.

SEMINOLE.   ENGLISH.

E-la-ni-ka-so-swaw ....Toe nail.
Chaw-taw..Blood.
Chaw-tee-fo-kaw.....................................Vein or artery.
Istee-e-kol-pee ....Brain (man).
E-kol-pee..Brain.
E-ho-sil-waw...Bladder.
E-fee-caw...Heart.
E-pof-caw..Around the heart.
E-to-chee ....Kidney
Iu-hee-shock-e-taw ....Lung.
E-lo-pee ....Liver.
Im-pa-shaw ....Stomach.
In-ta-law..Rib.
Iu-ka-shock-a-tee ....Pulse.
Es-tel-e-hop-o.......................................Foot print.
Shon-aw-haft-bee....................................Skin.
Shon-aw-fon-ee ....Bone.
Fix-chee-e-la-pots-kee.............................Intestines.
Cho-pock-e-taw.....................................Scalp.

Dress and Ornaments.

Cot-to-po-kaw.......................................Cap.
E-kof-kaw..Breech cloth.
She-won-nock-e-taw...............................Breech cloth belt.
Aw-fa-tee-kaw.......................................Leggins.
Stil-i-pi-kaw ....Moccasins.
Som-po-chee ....Basket.
Ech-e-taw..Blanket.
Lo-cus-haft-ee-pa-ta-kaw ....Bear skin (robe).
E-cho-haft-ee-pa-ta-kaw ....Deer skin (robe).
Cho-see..Buck skin or snake skin.
Cho-fee-haft-bee ....Rabbit skin.
O-sho-aw-haft-bee..................................Beaver skin.
O-shon-aw-haft-bee ....Otter skin.
Co-lo-waw..Paint.
Co-lo-waw-la-nee ....Paint (yellow).
Co-lo-wa-lus-tee ....Paint (black).

SEMINOLE.	ENGLISH.
Co-lo-wa-chaw-tee	Paint (red).
Shoke-shot-ta-pix-chee	Pouch.
Stink-ko-shot-ti-tee-caw	A ring,
Cop-a-to-ca-och-a-co	Bare head.
Es-tel-e-pi-e-ca-och-a-co	Bare foot.
E-ca-e-pee	Naked.
She-won-nock-e-ta-sa-lof-kaw	Knife belt.
Co-na-waw	Beads.
Hi-ef-cof-ka-taw	Shirt.
Stil-a-pa-won-bee	Shoes.
Note tes-chee	Handkerchief.
Es-ti-ha-kee	Picture.
Osh-aw-kil-caw-e-fa-caw	Watch chain.
Osh-aw-kil-caw	Watch.
She-ma-caw	Fan.
Shit-ta-kee-caw	Walking cane.

Dwellings, Implements, Utensils, Etc.

Cho-co-ta-ti-yee	Village.
Cho-co-hum-co-see	Wigwam.
E-how-kee	Door way.
We-chow-hi-lit	Spark.
No-clit	Burn.
Tode-caw	Fire.
Tock-hot-chee	Fire wood (burning).
Lip-la-it	Blaze.
Toke-la-waw	Living coals.
Tock-ees-so	Ashes.
Eh-cho-chee	Smoke.
Aw-lock-a-taw-chaw-ho-tee	My home.
Aw-ho-gee	Door way.
Pa-ta-caw	Bed.
Shot-hote-caw	Door.
Cho-ko	House.
Ko-lo-kee	Lamp.
Osh-aw-kil-caw-lock-o	Clock.
To-paw	Floor.

SEMINOLE.	ENGLISH.
Cho-ko-no-paw	Ceiling.
Cho-ko-shaw-hose-paw-caw	Wall.
Ot-so-caw	Stairway.
We-wa-ese-pay-lot-caw	Spring.
We-wa	Water.
E-pee-lo-faw	Hommock (woods).
E-con-aw-aw-ho-pa-caw	Map.
See-la-hot-tit-taw	Railing.
Tode-ca-e-ho-tee	Stove.
We-wa-ho-tee	Water tank.
Ho-e-so-clope-pa-lock-a-naw	Wash bowl.
In-ka-e-to-shi-ects-caw	Towel.
To-how-how-waw	Trunk.
So-cose-caw	Soap.
Sin-ti-ne-ta-pi-ee to-caw	Whisk broom.
Ees-cos-caw	Comb.
E-fa-ko-lock-o	Rope (cable).
Shot-hit-go-chee	Glass tumbler.
Tose-to-lese-taw	Wagon.
Tose-to-lese-ta-pof-na-chee	Buggy.
Aw-ta-lit-taw	Clothes hooks.
E-shaw-ho-tee	Gun cover.
Chot-a-dox-cha-in-chee	Arrow.
Bith-low	Canoe.
Sar-sho-e-fa-caw	Fish line.
Whe-ah	Fish net.
Hi-ects-caw	Accordeon.
Tock-kee-so	Ashes.
Buch es-waw	Ax.
Polk-ko	Pottery.
Le-ho-chaw	Pot of pottery.
Chat-o-lon-ee	Brass.
Che-to-ko-lope-lon-ee	Gold.
Sha-teck-e-naw-yaw	Silver.
Shot-to	Iron.
Hi-lo-chee	Cup.
We-wa-sis-ca-taw	Dipper.

SEMINOLE.	ENGLISH.
Sto-caw	Bucket.
E-slof-ka-pee	Knife handle.
E-slof-ka e-ock-shaw	Knife point.
E-slof-ka-e-in-fos-kee	Knife edge.
Sa-lof-ka	Knife.
Chum-chaw-cha-lock-ko	Bell.
Chum-chaw-ko	Small bell.
Shif-fon-waw	Awl.
To-shay-sil-caw	Whang (for sewing moccasins).
We-hop-caw	Pillow.
To-hi-o-waw	Valise.
To-ho-to-waw	Powder.
Ho-tee	Powder can.
Shaw-toke-e-naw-waw	Money.
To-ko-naw-shaw-tee	One cent.
Na-kop-po-chee	Ten cents.
Con-shot-go-ho-ko-lin	Fifty cents.
Chalk	Twenty-five cents.
To-ko-naw-wa-hum-kin	One dollar.
To-ko-naw-wa-cha-kee-bin	Five dollars.
E-sho-gaw	File.
Ees-how-ees-caw	Key.
Ees-pas-caw	Broom.
Chot-to-go-chee	Mallet.
Op-pee	Broomstick.
Tock-o-take-go-chee	Common stick.
Im-mi-lay-sha-taw	Court plaster.
Tose-ka-lof-caw	Plane.
E-to	Wood.
Tock-kin-o-shaw	Brick.
Ok-e-fots-chay	Sea shell.
To-hop-kee	Fence
Ho-lo-paw	Walk (pavement)
Chat-o-ko-cho	Cartridge.
Hi-ects-e-fa-caw	Guitar string.
O-like-a-taw	Chair.
To-paw	Floor.

SEMINOLE.	ENGLISH.
Es-ti-ha-kee	Picture.
Tol-lo-faw	Town.
Ist-fon-o-kee-taw	Rocking chair.
E-skil-caw	Compass.
Shock-shaw-e-taw	Dip net.
Ti-sos-so-chee	Pin.
Ees-la-pode-caw	Needle.
Ees-ti-no-tee-some-fo-tee-taw	Tooth pick.
Shoke-chaw	Sack.
It-to-tee-ish-fo-gaw	Ice saw.
It-to-tee-butch-es-waw	Ice hatchet.
It-to-tee-in-so-go	Ice house.
It-to-tee saw-gaw	Ice machine.
It-to-tee-ock-les-waw	Ice moulds.
It-to-tee-she-lot-caw	Ice tongs.
It-to-tee-we-waw	Ice water.
To-fo-ga-ta-leg-a-mee	Saw dust.
To-fo-la-hi-lee	Cord wood
To-to-lese-pof-a-naw-o-cho-go	Railroad car.
Phon-e-o-hop-ee	Fishing pole.
Sho-a-los-ga-taw	Hammock (to swing).
Ko-lo-kee-e-ho-tee	Lantern.
Tol-lot-to-chee	Brush.
O-pa-tock-o	Saddle.
E-ho-e-lit-taw	Stirrup.
She-lop-ko-chif-ko-taw	Spur.
Ach-aw-kil-caw-lock-o	Clock.
E-sho-e-caw	Hoe.
Hot-cus-waw	Iron kettle.
Ta-pate-go-chee	Pistol.
Ich-chaw	Gun.
E-chaw	Rifle.
To-lo-to-lon-e	Cap (percussion).
To-hote-to-waw	Powder.
Wee-aw	Seine.
Sa-lof-ka-chop-ka	Sword.
Sa-lof-ka-chee	Knife (small).

SEMINOLE.	ENGLISH.
Sa-lof ka-fots-kee	Knife (sharp).
Sa-lof-ka-tof-nee	Knife (dull).

Food.

SEMINOLE.	ENGLISH.
To-lee-ko	Oatmeal.
O-chee-tot-o-la-go-chee	Corn bread.
Tot-o-lo-som-po-chee	Cake.
Pish-waw	Meat.
O-po-swaw	Soup.
Tock-a-la-kee	Bread (flour).
Och-chee-lo-wat-kee	Corn (green).
Wa-ka-pish-aw	Milk.
Chum-pee	Honey.
Yel-la-haw	Lemonade
Fo-chum-pee	Bees and honey.
Ist-sa-tock-ko	Cauliflower.
O-ko-to	Radish.
Oke-chou-tel-o-ko-nee	Salt.
Il-la-haw	Orange.
Itch-on-e-haw	Tallow.
Ho-waw	Pepper sauce.
E-cho-pish-waw	Deer meat.
Chil-i-hos-waw	Pineapple.
Wa-ka-pish-aw-tock-o-la-kee	Cheese.
Tol-o-so-caw	Cocoanut.
Chos-chee-lock-o	Pumpkin (white man's).
Chos-chee	Pumpkin (Indian).
E-po-see-waw	Gravy.
Fit-chee	Sausage.
We-len-tel-lo	Banana.
Hil-o-cho-waw	Chewing gum.
Wa-ka-pish-a-ne-haw	Butter.
Wa-ka-pish-e-e-tok-chee	Sour milk.
Wa-ka-fit-chee	Sausage (beef).
Suck-a-fit-chee	Sausage (pork).
Ho-tes-kot-tee-hot-kee	Flour.
Whit-lo-ko	Oysters.

SEMINOLE.	ENGLISH.
Aw-haw	Potato (sweet).
Tol-o-la-go-chee	Biscuit.
Aw-hot-to-pox-to-chee	Potato (Irish).
Cot-lo-chee	Sardines.
Aw-pis-ta-lake-a-to-me	Potted ham.
Tock-a-la-kee-chom-paw	Ginger cake (large).
Ho-maw	Pickles.
Pe-kon-o-soch-o-chee	Cherries.
Tock-a-fon-waw	Filbert.
Shot-o-lock-o	Apple.
Chil-loos-wa	Grapes.
Tock-a-la-kee-chum-po-chee	Cake (small).

Colors.

Lus-tee	Black.
Ho-lot-tee	Blue.
Ho-ko-lon-i-tee	Brown.
Sho-po-ka-hot-ka-chee	Grey.
Pi-e-lon-o-maw	Green.
Chat-tee	Red.
Hot-ka-tee	White.

Numerals.

Hum-kin	One.
Ho-ko-lin	Two.
Too-chin	Three.
Os-tin	Four.
Chaw-kee-bin	Five.
A-pa-kin	Six.
Ko-lo-pa-kin	Seven.
Chin-na-pa-kin	Eight.
Os-ta-pa-kin	Nine.
Pa-lin	Ten.
Pa-lin-hum-kin-hum-kin	Eleven.
Pa-lin-hum-kin-ho-ko-lin	Twelve.
Pa-lin-hum-kin-too-chin	Thirteen.

SEMINOLE.	ENGLISH.
Pa-lin-hum-kin-os-tin	Fourteen.
Pa-lin-ho-ko-lin	Twenty.
Pa-lin-ho-ko-lin-hum-kin	Twenty-one.
Pa-lin-ho-ko-lin-too-chin	Twenty-three.
Pa-lin-too-chin	Thirty.
Pa-lin-os-tin	Forty.
Pa-lin-chaw-kee-bin	Fifty.
Pa-lin-a-pa-kin	Sixty.
Pa-lin-ko-la-pa-kin	Seventy.
Pa-lin-chin-na-pa-kin	Eighty.
Pa-lin-os-ta-pa-kin	Ninety.
Chope-kee-hum-kin	One hundred.
Chope-kee-ho-ko-lin	Two hundred.
Chope-kee-too-chin-ee	Three hundred.

Divisions of Time.

Ti-ose-go-chee	First moon (August).
Ti-ose-go-lock-o	Second moon (September).
E-ho-lee	Third moon (October).
Si-lof-slop-ko	Fourth moon (November).
Si-lof-so-kee	Fifth moon (December).
Ho-ti-lee-has-ee	Sixth moon (January).
Ti-sot-to-chee	Seventh moon (February).
Ti-sot-to-lock-o	Eighth moon (March).
Kee-hos-ee	Ninth moon (April).
Got-so-hos-ee	Tenth moon (May).
Hi-yote-chee	Eleventh moon (June).
Hi-yote-lock-o	Twelfth moon (July).
Mis-kee-hum-kin	One year.
Ha-lits-chey	Moon.
Nit-taw	Day.
Nist-lee	Night.
U-mus-ka-taw	Dark.
Pox-son-gay	Yesterday.
Pox-son-gay-lim-pix-son-gay	Day before yesterday.
A-pox-see-lim-pox-say-nist-lee	Day after to-morrow night.
Mo-shon-nit-taw	To-day.

SEMINOLE.	ENGLISH.
A-pox-see	To-morrow.
A-pox-see lim-pox-say	Day after to-morrow.
Mis-kee-hum-kee	Next year.
Mo-shon-mis-kee	This year.
Mis-kee-ho-ko-lin	Two years.
Mis-kee-too-chin-aw	Three years.
Nit-ti-chow-go-hum-kin	One week.
Nit-ti-chow-go-ho-ko-lin	Two weeks.
Nit-ti-chow-go-too-chin-aw	Three weeks.
Nit-ta-hum-kin	One day.
Nit-ta-ho-ko-liu	Two days.
Nit-ta-too-chin-aw	Three days.
Nit-ta-os-tin	Four days.
Mo-shon-nist-lee	To night.
A-pox-see-nist-lee	To-morrow night.
Mo-cho-hos-see	This moon.
Hos-see-hum-kee	Next moon.
Osh-aw-kil-hum-kin	One o'clock.
Osh aw-kil-ho-ko-lin	Two o'clock.

Animals, Parts of Body, etc.

Lo-ko-see	Bear (black).
Ko-wat-go-chee	Cat (wild).
E-faw	Dog.
E-cho	Deer.
Chil-la	Fox.
E-cho-wa-a-taw	Goat (mountain).
Su-caw-pin-si-law	Hog (wild).
E-chos-waw	Manatee or sea cow.
Tock-o	Mole.
O-shen-aw	Otter.
Su-caw-hot-caw	Opossum.
Ches-she	Rat.
Cho-fee	Rabbit.
Cho-fee-chaw-hot-ee	Rabbit (grey).
Wood-ko	Raccoon.
Klo-hi-lee	Squirrel.

SEMINOLE.	ENGLISH.
Klo-hot-go-chee	Squirrel (grey).
Klo-hi-lee-chaw-tee	Squirrel (red).
Yee-haw	Wolf.
Kon-kla-po-chee	Chameleon.
E-cho-yi-pee	Antlers.
Wa-ka-e-fo-nce	Bone (cow).
Fit-chee-law-pots-kee	Entrails.
Nee-haw	Fat.
Wa-ka-haft-bee	Hide (cow).
Yi-pee	Horn.
Fit-chee-lock-o	Stomach.
E-hot-chee	Tail.
E-no-tee	Teeth.
E-po-lo-wa-kee	Elephant.
Chil-lock-o	Horse.
Chil-lock-o-chee	Colt.
Chil-lock-o-pi-e-caw	Mule.
Wal-ka-ho-non-waw	Ox.
Wal-ka-chee	Calf.
Suck-aw	Hog.
Po-sha-chee	Cat.
Yep-e-fa-e-caw	Sheep.
E-fa-chee	Puppy.
Cho-wa-taw	Goat.
Wal-ka	Cow.

Birds.

O-so-waw	Bird.
O-chot-aw	Black bird.
Shock-kil law	Black bird (red wing).
Wa-to-law	Whooping crane.
O-shaw-o-waw	Crow.
Hi-lo-lo	Curlew.
Hi-lo-lo-chaw-tee	Curlew (pink).
Posh-e-ho-we	Dove.
Fo-cho	Duck.
Hat-tit-e-fon-caw	Eagle.

SEMINOLE.	ENGLISH.
Sho-caw	Hawk.
Sho-ko-chee	Sparrow hawk.
Hos-cho-kee waw	Fish hawk.
Wak-ko-lot-ko	Heron (great blue).
Wak-ko-lot-ko-o-hi-lot-tee	Heron (little blue).
Fost-chi-taw	Red bird.
Hi-lo-lo	Ibis (white).
Tos-chee	Jay (blue).
Pen-na-waw	Turkey.
We-hot-ko-fo-sho-wo-chee	Snipe.
Eash-pock-a-waw	Robin.
Fost-chi-taw	Red bird.
Sho-lee	Vulture.
Sho-lee-pee-los-pes-ko	Vulture (black).
Chip-ee-lop-law	Whippoorwill.
Fo-a-kee	Quail.
Pen-nit-kee	Turkey hen.
Pen-na-waw-en-to-wee	Turkey beard.
Pen-cha-ho-gaw	Turkey cry.
Pen-ni-chaw	Turkey gobbler.
Fo-shon-nits-kaw	Rookery.
Shee	Feathers.
Lo-cha-e-stow-cha-kee	Egg.
O-cho-ko	King fisher.
Ho-shock-e-a-caw	Limkin.
O-shi-hi-yi	Mocking bird.
E-fo-law	Owl (screech).
Pot-see-lon-ee	Paroquet.
To-to-lo-chee	Chicken.
O-shot-caw	Heron (great white).
O-shot-co-chee	Heron (little white).
O-pal	Owl (eared).
E-chee-pa-hot-tee	Mother Cary's chicken (Petrel).

Fish and Reptiles.

Sar-sho	Fish.
Sar-sho-o-kee-lon-waw	Cat fish.

SEMINOLE.	ENGLISH.
Whit-lo-ko……. ……………………………	Oyster.
Shar-lo…. …………………………………………	Trout.
Sar-sho-chee…………………… ………………	Minnow.
Shup-sho-chee …………………………………	Pickerel.
Al-la-pa-taw……………………………………	Alligator.
Aw-pa-to-naw.…………………………………	Frog.
Chit-ta-mic-co……………………… } or {	Chief of snakes.
Chit-ko-la-la-go-chee……………… } {	Rattle snake.
Ko-tee………………………………………………	Toad.
Chit-ta-lus-tee.…………………………………	Black snake.
Aw-shock-o-law ………………………………	Snail.
Ho lock-waw.……………………………………	Turtle (soft shell).
Lo-chaw……….. …………………………………	Turtle (land).
Chit-ta-lock-a-chee …………………………	Snake (spotted).
O-co-la-chit ta.…………………………………	Snake (green).
Skin-cho-caw …………………………………	Frog (tree).
Gotch-es-waw…………………………………	Turtle.

Insects.

Tock-o-cha-cha-tee……. ………………………	Aut (red).
Tock-o-cha-lus-tee …………………………	Aut (black).
Fo-a ………………………………………………	Bee.
Chil-lock-o-fo-a ……………………………	Bee (drone).
Cuff-ko …………………………………………	Flea.
Cho-naw ………………………………………	Fly.
Scop-o-swaw …………………………………	Gnat
A-caw-ko-taw ………………………………	Grasshopper.
Chil-lock-o-do-no ……………………………	Horse fly.
Taw-fo …………………………………………	Katy-did.
O-he-aw…………………………………………	Mosquito.
Och-klo-klou …………………………………	Spider.
U-c-cot-taw …………………………………	Worm.
Och-o-klon-we-ahr …………………………	Spider web.
To-ka-tes-kee-at-tee-lo-e-waw ………………	Silk worm.
Soke-so …………………………………………	Beetle (black).

Plants.

SEMINOLE.	ENGLISH.
Lock-e-tum-ba-e-cec	Oak leaf.
Ech-to-fa-la-ha-lee	Chip.
E-to	Wood (to burn).
Cho-lee-saw	Pine leaf.
Im-pock-pock-ee	Flower.
Pi-hee	Grass.
Gatch-ho-ho-e-claw	Blackberry.
Aw-won-aw	Willow tree.
Chit-ta-hum-pe-ta	Snake plant.
Til-e-ko	Oats.
Shot-i-pee	Persimmon tree.
Shot-taw	Persimmon.
Shot-o-nin-kla	Persimmon seed.
Gotch-o	Poison vine.
Aw-shen-lock-o	Air plant.
Aw-shen-waw	Moss
Shil o-fo-haw	Water lily.
We-sho	Sassafras.
Tol-o-lock-o	Palmetto (cabbage tree).
Tol-o-chee	Palmetto (young cabbage tree).
Tol-o-neck-la	Palmetto seed.
She-hop-paw	Saw palmetto.
Aw-shit-ta-taw	Gall berries.
Aw-tock-claw	Weed.
Chaw-fo-ka-naw	Huckleberries.
Hi-lis-hot-kee	Ginseng.
He-swan-i-hit-caw	Quinine.
Gout-lock-o	Cactus.
Com-to-lock-o	Peanut.
Ti-fum-bee	Onion.
Hee-chee	Tobacco.
O-chee-o-pee	Hickory tree.
Kee	Mulberry tree.
Hatch-in-e-haw	Cypress tree.
E-la-hock-o	Shaddock (grape fruit).

The Firmament—Physical Phenomena, Etc.

SEMINOLE   ENGLISH.

Go-chee-som-po-lock-o............................Large star.
Go-chee-som-pol-e-poch-go-chee.............Small star.
Cho-go-lof-caw ....Seven stars.
Ho-nit-claw ....North star.
Wa-hit-law...South star.
Ho-so-shaw ....East star.
Aw-kil-lot-caw ....West star.
Ha-shay ....Sun.
Hit-to-tee.. Frost.
It-to-tee ....Ice.
We-wa..Water.
Os-e-caw ....Rain.
Ti-nit-kee ....Thunder.
Ot-to-e-hot-tit ....Lightning.
Go-ti-lee...Wind.
Ha-notch-e-fo-law ....Whirlwind.
E ho-tee...Ground.
O-ti-lee-lock-o ....Storm.
Ha-shay-shay-pock-taw-lo-gaw ....Eclipse of the sun.
Ho-nit-chaw ....North.
Ha-so-saw ....East.
Wa-ha-law ....South.
Op-a-lock-aw..West.
Ha-lits cha-shay-pock-ta-lo-gaw ....Eclipse of the moon.
Hi-yi-tee-e-chaw ....Morning star.
E-pof-kee ....Evening.
Hi-e-ta-ma-es-chee................................Heat.
Chit-cho..Dew.
Ho-lo-chee ....A cloud.

Kinship.

Sop-po-chee ....My son.
Chat-hos-tee...My daughter.
Solk-go-chee ....My father.
Sots-kee ....My mother.
E-chock-o-tee................................... ...Brother.
E-cho-see..Brother (younger).

SEMINOLE.	ENGLISH.
E-la-ha	Brother (older).
Cho-wen-waw	Sister.
Cha-hi-e-waw	My wife.
Squaw	Wife
Picc-a-nin-ny	Child.

Verbs, Phrases, Sentences.

Ah-ho-chee	To plant
Tote-ca-taw	To whistle.
E-lo-chaw	To date.
Lop-ko	Make haste.
Ah-mos-chay	To give.
Chim-moc-co-dos-chay	Not to give.
Hum-bi-da-lon-es-chay	To feed.
Yi-es-chay	To sell.
Neich-hi-es-chee	Not to buy
Hock-ka-cet-kit	To cry.
Op-peel-it	To laugh.
E-hi-e-kit	To sing.
Fi-i-it-lot-es chee	To hunt.
Oh-in-i-it	To smell.
Clot-la-klip-chay	To break.
Sop-pa-lon-es-chay	To sleep.
He-ches-chee	To see.
Im-po-hos-chee	To hear.
Ah-es-chay	Go.
Hi-e pus	To go.
Chi-yot-chit	To like.
Aw-lock-chay	To come.
Cha-ho-sit	Forgot.
O-ko-sit	Wash.
He-chus-chee	Saw.
Fit-kon-nit	Wait.
Hal-wuk	It is bad.
Hink-las	It is good.
Hi-o-e-pus-chay	Two go.
Hi-op-pee-pox-es-chay	Three or more go.

SEMINOLE.	ENGLISH.
I-wox-chee	Many come.
Aw-mul-cay	All come.
No-chip-os-chay	Go sleep (you).
Clot-la-klip-chay	Broken (to break).
Sup-pa-lou-es-chay	I take.
Chi-ho-ches-chee	I am lost.
Che-ho-shar	You are lost.
E-wa-kee-pa-lon-es-chay	Lie down, but not to sleep.
Hum-kin-mi-si-e-pit	Take one.
Ye-hi-e-pa-taw	To sing.
So-toke-kee-na-aw-aw-mun-chee	Give me money.
Hi-e-pus-chay	I go.
Ot-som-ka-taw	To go up steps.
Hi-top-ka-taw	To go down steps.
Hock-it	To whistle.
Cho-ho-sit	Forgot.
Chi-yot-chec	I want.
E-see-op-cop-e-taw	To ride.
Chee-yi-chee	Do you want?
Mot-to	Thank you.
Es-tel-e-pi-e-ka-u-cha-ko-ot-e-he	To put moccasins on.
Kit-lix-chay	Don't know.
Kit-li-es-chay	I know.
Aw-kay-lot-kit	Go in.
Lop-ko-sin-ot-tos-chay	Come quick.
Chee-to-gaw	To pole a boat.
Scof-gaw	To row a boat.
Hum-pux-chay-hum-pee-taw	You eat plenty.
No-chee-pa-lon-es-chay	I am going to sleep.
Sa-lof-ka-chop-kaw	My knife is large (sword).
Sa-lof-ka-chee	My knife is small.
A-pok-es-chay	All sit down.
No-chip-os-chay	Go sleep (you).
Che-mo-on-ot-es-chay	Are you sleepy?
I-hoo-es-chay	Let us go.
Ho	Yes.
Li-kus-chay	Sit down.

SEMINOLE.	ENGLISH.
Hi-top-cay-ta-li-kus-chay	Sit down on steps.
No-chit-pay-lon-es-chay	Lie down and sleep.
Its-kec-e-i-chce-tok-naw	Mother wants to keep him.
In-ka-o-ko-sit	Wash hands.
Mi-e-taw	Tall (tree).
Che-mi-hee	Grow (you or me).
Che-mi-hce-ta-mi-hee cha-mi-he-taw	Grow very tall.
Aw-ne-chec-mi-he-taw	I grow.
I-ti-it-tot-chi-mi-he-taw-mi-he-taw-te-hee	I will grow tall.
Ha-tec-e-tew-chee-hick-chay-hit-es-chay	Glad to see you.
E-cho-lid-kit-he-chus-chee	I saw deer run.
E-cho-ti-een-lid-kit-he-chus-chee	I saw deer run fast.
E-cho-lid-kit-smi-hi-ko-in-iu-he-chus-chee	I saw deer run slow.
E-cho-yak-op-po-sit	Deer walk.
E-cho-yak-op-po-sit-hi-chus-chee	I saw the deer walk.
E-cho-mo-chon-it-ta-we-wa-ah-kay-lot-kit-o-mi-e-it-i-in-he-chus-chee	To-day I saw a deer go in the water and swim.
Il-lich-is-caw	Did you kill it?
Lop-fi-eets-chay	Let us hunt.
Iu-po-hitch-caw	Do you hear?
He-chos-kos-chay	I can't find it.
To-pa-li-kus-chay	Sit on floor (you).
Pish-wa-chi-us-chee	I want some meat.
Aw-som-es-chee-aw-pish-waw	Pass me the meat.
Lox-a-dox-chay	You lie.
Is-chay-to-ma-es-chce	Wind blew hard.
He-a-maw	Come here.
Suck-chay	All gone.
Aw-pok-es-chay	All sit down.
Ha-sha-col-lock-tit	Sun gone down.
Ha-sha-i-sit	Sun come up.
To-ko-naw-yo-ko-dos-chay	Money, no sell'em.
On-e-way	Me too.
Un-gaw	All right.
Nock-a-tee	What is it?
Stom-a-taw	Which way?

SEMINOLE.	ENGLISH.
Aw-lip-ka-shaw	Good-by.
Aw-tee-tus-chee	By-and-by.
Ho-lo-wa-gus	No good.
Hi-lip-pit-ka-shaw	How are you?
Som-mus-ka-lar-nee-shaw	Good luck.
Ya-maw	This way.
Hock-es-chee	Bird cry.
Chi-yot-chit	Like them.
Chee	Young or small.
O-fun-net-taw	Long time.
En-cha-mun chay	Well or good.
Ho-nit-chay,	Wild.
Ni-hit-tus-chay	Fat.
Wi-o-kee-tus-chay	Poor.
Es-to-chee-hock-a-effee	Baby cry.
E-yof-kee-hum-pee-taw	Supper (before dark).
E-mots-kee-hum-pee-taw	Supper (after dark).
Kan-yuk-sa-es-ta-chat-tee	Florida red men.
Yo-ho-ee-hee	War whoop.
Aw-pox-see-lim-pox-say-nist-lee	Day after to-morrow night.
Stu-es-taw	A great deal, or too much.
Ya-ti-ka-chic-co	Great Speaker (Commissioner.)
Munks-chay	No.
Hi-lit-la-ma-es-chay	Too hot (fire-water).
Im-e-lo-la-tee-ti-yee	Water rough.
Ko-no-wa-hum-kin-mo-so-nit-ta-wi-yy- ches-chee	} I want a string of beads to-day.
Shot-cay-taw	Green Corn Dance.
In-like-e-taw	Heaven.
E-shock-e-tom-e-see	The Supreme Ruler or the white man's God.
E-shock-e-tom-e-see-e-po-chee	God's son, Christ.
His-a-kit-a-mis-i	Great Spirit.
Po-ya-fits-a	Indian's heaven.
Il-lit	Death.
Som-mus-ka-lar-nee-sha-maw-lin	Good wishes to white man.

The Indian Names of Some Present Seminoles.

Tallahassee ....Mic-co.
So-fan-gee ....Mi-la-kee.
Fi-lan-e-hee ....Tal-la-has-so-wee.
Las-ches-chee ....Fo-ston-sto-noc-ee-la.
Ko-i-hat-cho.......................................Cal-lo-fo-nee.
Yee-ho-lo-chee ....Tol-lo-see.
O-mul-la-gee .... .Shon-o-la-kee.
She-y-o-hee...On-nit-chee.
Sla-shing-to-goth-la-gee.......................I-o-chus-chee.
Che-e-ho-la ....Suck-kin-ho-chee.
Sten-o-la-kee ....Os-ce-o-la.
Cho-fee-hat-cho ....Mat-lo.
Os-shen-e-ho-la ....Nan-ces-o-wee.
Ho-puth-tee-na-gee..............................Tal-lem-ee.
Tin-fai-yai-ki ....Kat-ca-la-ni.

www.ingramcontent.com/pod-product-compliance
Lightning Source LLC
Chambersburg PA
CBHW021131020726
47500CB00003B/1030